"To thrive, the church can't merely be about making converts, but must focus its energies on making *disciples*—the very essence of the Great Commission. *Real Life* is a huge step in the right direction, offering a simple, practical tool to help everyone involved in disciplemaking to know that the objective is to get disciples to walk, talk, think, feel and do as Jesus did. For the sake of the church, read this book and put it into action!"

DOUG BIRDSALL, executive chair, Lausanne Committee for World Evangelization

"The artificial—and inaccurate—dichotomy between discipleship and evangelism has been deadly to the church. This book by James Choung is a worthy antidote. It is practical. It is missional. It moves followers of Jesus toward a life of depth and significance and living out the good news for the long haul. It is for anyone seriously desiring to live as an authentic disciple and, in turn, help others in the journey of following Jesus."

SAM METCALF, president, Church Resource Ministries-U.S.

"This is the real deal, folks. Like a good story, *Real Life* draws you in—it is honest and elegant and helps you understand yourself and your world better. And like a good tool, *Real Life* empowers you—it is solid and practical and helps you work more fruitfully. In the important task of disciplemaking in the twenty-first century, the church desperately needs stories and tools like this."

DON EVERTS, author of *Go and Do: Becoming a Missional Christian* and *I Once Was Lost: What Postmodern Skeptics Taught Us About Their Path to Jesus*

"A discipleship adventure and story you won't want to put down! The Real Life Continuum is a simple but powerful vision of what discipleship could be and should be. Choung brilliantly narrates a model that impacts deeply and broadly, from skeptics to world changers. It's a must-read for anyone exploring disciplemaking."

TOM LIN, director, Urbana Student Missions Conference, vice president, InterVarsity Christian Fellowship/USA

"*Real Life* changes the paradigm for disciplemaking the way *True Story* pushed evangelism beyond the bridge diagram. Choung weaves an engaging story with helpful data, explains cultural and generational values and shifts, and moves us into the core spiritual questions of each generation. *Real Life* asks readers to consider disciplemaking as part of integrated Christian life and leadership in community without separating it from evangelism. I'm excited to see how the church will live and grow after reading *Real Life.*"

KATHY KHANG, multiethnic director, Great Lakes West Region, InterVarsity Christian Fellowship, and coauthor, *More Than Serving Tea*

"In fresh, clear, 'talking to you straight' language, Choung tells an intriguing story to encourage people who want more in their spiritual life. He paints a compelling and accessible picture of what a full life in Christ looks like. He explains the dynamics we see but can't quite put into words—and then he goes on to give insightful, practical and compelling next steps. He connects elusive topics such as race, power and privilege with familiar ones such as prayer, Scripture study and church. An excellent resource for those wanting more in their experience with God and for leaders of faith communities! A surprisingly powerful book, crammed into a small, readable package."

NIKKI TOYAMA-SZETO, Urbana program director, coauthor of *Partnering with the Global Church*

"Choung tells the story of discipleship in such a way that the most hesitant will be motivated to get off the couch to be and make disciples of Jesus. Because he paints a picture of discipleship through story, the lessons linger with you long after you shut the pages of the book."

JR WOODWARD, cofounder, Ecclesia Network, author, *Creating a Missional Culture*

"Practical, wise, inspiring. James Choung is a gifted storyteller. *Real Life: A Christianity Worth Living Out* teaches biblical principles in discipleship via an entertaining story about Stephen, a young professional who desires to see God's presence in the everyday realities of his family, vocation and relationships. Choung introduces the Real Life Continuum, an extremely helpful framework for the discipleship journey."

ALEC HILL, president, InterVarsity Christian Fellowship/USA

REAL LIFE

A Christianity Worth Living Out

JAMES CHOUNG

IVP Books

An imprint of InterVarsity Press
Downers Grove, Illinois

InterVarsity Press
P.O. Box 1400, Downers Grove, IL 60515-1426
World Wide Web: www.ivpress.com
E-mail: email@ivpress.com

©2012 by James Choung

InterVarsity Press® is the book-publishing division of InterVarsity Christian Fellowship/ USA®, a movement of students and faculty active on campus at hundreds of universities, colleges and schools of nursing in the United States of America, and a member movement of the International Fellowship of Evangelical Students. For information about local and regional activities, write Public Relations Dept., InterVarsity Christian Fellowship/USA, 6400 Schroeder Rd., P.O. Box 7895, Madison, WI 53707-7895, or visit the IVCF website at <www.intervarsity.org>.

All Scripture quotations, unless otherwise indicated, are taken from the Holy Bible, New International Version®. NIV®. Copyright ©1973, 1978, 1984 by International Bible Society. Used by permission of Zondervan Publishing House. All rights reserved.

While all stories in this book are true, some names and identifying information in this book have been changed to protect the privacy of the individuals involved.

Cover design: Cindy Kiple
Images: Frederick Bass/Getty Images
Interior design: Beth Hagenberg

ISBN 978-0-8308-3654-3

Printed in the United States of America ∞

 green press INITIATIVE InterVarsity Press is committed to protecting the environment and to the responsible use of natural resources. As a member of Green Press Initiative we use recycled paper whenever possible. To learn more about the Green Press Initiative, visit <www.greenpressinitiative.org>.

Library of Congress Cataloging-in-Publication Data has been requested.

P	16	15	14	13	12	11	10	9	8	7	6	5	4	3	2	1
Y	25	24	23	22	21	20	19	18	17	16	15	14	13	12		

To Nathan—

Seek first his kingdom

and his righteousness.

Everything else will be given.

CONTENTS

BEFORE WE START

If you remain in me and I in you, you will bear
much fruit; apart from me you can do nothing.

Jesus, John 15:5

Doug is one of my closest friends on the planet—though, given our differences, he really shouldn't be. I grew up in the city. He grew up on a farm. I'm in full-time ministry. He's a full-time military officer. I'm a flaming extrovert, while he can be happy buried in his books. I'm a skinny Korean guy of average height. At six-foot-four, he's a gentler, sandy-brown-haired version of Gaston in *Beauty and the Beast.* Politically, our debates can get heated. But among the things we have in common, we've both played far too much *Goldeneye* on the Nintendo 64. And we both love Jesus and try to live out our faith each day.

Our faith drew us together when Doug moved to Boston for graduate school and found a spiritual home in our newly planted church. Since then, we've supported each other through relational ups and downs, and he was instrumental in keeping me sane through my crisis of faith. We stood or served in each other's weddings and became godfathers to each other's firstborn sons. It's a huge gift to have a friendship that I know will last the number of days we get to walk on the earth.

Recently we were hunched over his dining table, propped up on our elbows, talking again far too late into the night. He said that everyone in his church's small group had mourned recent losses. Some suffered pain *because of* their faithfulness to Jesus. They all had grown up in the church, but now, in their thirties, they found that their known spiritual routines provided little comfort or inspiration. In addition, Doug and his wife were both juggling time-consuming jobs while raising a towering giant of a toddler. Life was full and tough. With a sigh, Doug concluded, "We're just not sure what the kingdom is supposed to mean in our everyday lives."

Jesus wants us to remain in him. He repeated it so often that it's hard to miss his point: remaining in him is absolutely critical if we are to thrive in life. It's the difference between spiritual life and death. If we remain, we can bear much fruit. If we don't, we can do nothing. It doesn't get much plainer than that.

But what does it mean to *remain* today?

Some of us conjure the miraculous to show up on Sunday mornings with infants wailing in our arms. Others manage to eke out times between overtime hours and family pressures to participate in the communal life of a church small group. Sometimes we're given the strength to put down the textbooks and crack open our Bibles and pray. We do our best with what we have. Yet God still feels distant. Intimacy with God feels like an unkept promise.

In the haze, our spiritual lives can lack direction. The next steps seem unclear. It's like placing a runner in the middle of an open, grassy field and firing the starting gun, but there's no lane or path to sprint on. We yell, "Run!" but she stands paralyzed, not knowing where to go. In the same way, we wait, all the while wondering if a vibrant spiritual life is actually out of reach.

But why does the picture of the Christian life feel elusive and ephemeral? Shouldn't it just make sense? I don't mean that we'd have all the answers—far from it!—but perhaps we'd have at least a sense of what we're supposed to work on or rest in next? If remaining in Jesus is so crucial, why is it so hard to figure out?

It makes me wonder: Are we doing a good job of preparing the people of faith for the "long obedience in the same direction"? Are we possibly better at getting people to cross the starting line than getting them to break the tape at the finish? At our urging, our newly believing friends may start to read the Bible, pray each day and get plugged into Christian community. What happens after these rhythms fail to inspire? After a few years, will this remain a compelling picture of everyday life with Jesus for them?

Is it still compelling for us?

These questions lead to an even more fundamental one: What do we hope that every single Christian would be able to do or be? I'm not asking about the ideal of Christian perfection. The question is more toes-in-the-earth practical. What is the vision of life for the everyday Christian? It's a question about discipleship: What does it mean to be a follower of Jesus today? What would Jesus ask us to do and be, if he lived in our time and place? Our answers to this question—or the lack of helpful, concrete ones— could have a butterfly effect on our ability to develop and empower believers over the long haul.

I wonder if that's a big reason why many people start to lose spiritual vitality, even leaving what they've known as faith altogether: they don't have a practical vision of how their faith is supposed to develop today. So faith starts feeling irrelevant. As the old adage goes, if you aim at nothing, you'll hit it every single time. "Just let God love you" can feel too vague and irrelevant to convince people to stick it out. "Love God, love others" is a great summary—after all, Jesus said it—but it still could leave a believer without an understanding of how to be a Christian today in practical ways.

When we lack a clear vision of discipleship, the consequences are dire. It could be the difference between the eternal kind of life—real life—or apathy, if not outright rejection of faith. We need something more concrete, yet still simple enough to remember.

My first book, *True Story,* provided a new way to share the old gospel in postmodern times. This book is the next step: If we trust in the gospel, then how do we live it out today? How do we serve those who become believers and help them become mature followers of Jesus?

It would be a shame if after capturing a bigger and more biblical view of the gospel, and understanding the deep, deep goodness of our message, we went back to business as usual. A shift in the message should also produce a shift in the model. If we proclaim a faith that sends us out into the world—through the Spirit's leading—to be agents of healing, then our discipleship models should reflect that new understanding. If we call people to be "sent together to heal," but then on Sunday ask them to be small group leaders or to join the welcoming team, they may feel a strong disconnect without further explanation on how their participation in the church will be for the good of those beyond its walls. We will be speaking new things out of our mouths and yet still be doing old things with our actions. And we know that actions speak far louder than words.

Along these lines, this book is a discipleship book. But it also differs in a couple of ways. First, it's a discipleship model that starts well before someone actually comes to faith, breaking down a too-rigid dichotomy between evangelism and discipleship.

One friend attempted to bring the two together by saying, "We do evangelism because Jesus might come tomorrow, but we do discipleship because he probably won't." It's a funny quote, but even this idea divorces the two. Instead, what if our discipleship models included evangelism? What if these two were reconciled as deep partners of the same kind of thing: helping our friends—both unbelievers and believers—to trust Jesus more, to do what he did for the reasons he did them? That way, evangelism would merely be the early stages of discipleship for someone who is not yet a believer, and our witness could set our friends up well for a discipleship to come.

Second, this book attempts to go further than a contemplative model of discipleship and into the mission beyond the church. Dallas Willard once expressed, "In a pluralistic world, a religion is valued by the benefits it brings to its nonadherents." Thus, our discipleship models need to be more than just obtaining spiritual rhythms, or even merely becoming more like Jesus in his character, though these are great and needed things. Our practices of piety must connect to being salt and light in the world—not just at an individual level, but also in relational and societal ways as well.

This book is also a leadership book. It's not, however, solely about the tasks or skills of effective leadership. It's not even about the character of a leader alone. There are plenty of excellent books on that. Instead, it's about leadership development, about defining more precisely what we're trying to do when we mentor others. In other words, it's a book about disciplemaking. My hope is that discipleship and disciplemaking would flow as one river, to help all of God's people reflect a deeper Christian maturity and be of greater nourishment and refreshment to the world around them.

Following the pattern in *True Story,* we'll start with a fictional narrative. Particularly when it comes to discipleship, the narrative forces us to crawl out of the shadows of the abstract into the bright, revealing light of the practical. It also highlights a new disciplemaking model—the "Real Life Continuum"—and shines a spotlight on experiences, feelings, questions, applications and generational insights as the characters try to learn and live out portions of the model in an everyday setting. A picture may be worth a thousand words, but a story invites us to experience things firsthand. The shorter and final portion of the book will leave the story and tread back through the details of the Real Life Continuum in a more straightforward manner. I hope that two different angles on the same ideas will help bring greater clarity and thus be of greater service and usefulness.

All Christians are called to be disciples and make disciples. Yet the field-tested model in this book isn't a guarantee. If you're looking for a foolproof way to force people to grow in faith, this book isn't for you. Instead, its intent is to remain simple yet robust enough to give anyone—from high school student to retiree—a vision of what it means to grow and to mentor others into Christian maturity. And by offering greater clarity of what discipleship could be—and thus what the Christian life is about—I hope and pray that our friends find a Christianity worth living out and grow into the fullness of who they were always meant to be.

ONCE UPON A TIME (AGAIN)

PROLOGUE

Generations

CRASH

Stephen's eyes couldn't focus on the computer screen in front of him. He leaned forward in his office chair, banged the table with his fists and let out an unusually loud grunt. His boss's most recent words pounded between his temples like jungle drums:

Maybe until one or two in the morning. Could be later.

"Another late night," he grumbled to himself. It was the sixth one in the last two weeks. This time, one of their biggest clients had a problem with Mobiship's tracking systems: tens of thousands of shipments disappeared from the electronic manifests, and they weren't happy. It needed to be fixed right away, and since Stephen was the lead manager of that project, he and his team would need to debug the code and get the tracking system back online as soon as possible, even if that meant staying all night. To add insult to injury, the boss had already headed home.

He swiveled around his chair and glossed again over the notes he'd just written on the wall-to-wall whiteboard, looking for a clue. Then, distracted, he turned his head toward the side wall full of pastel sticky notes—the timeline for his current project. He grimaced as he realized how far behind schedule they were, even as they prepared to stay the night to troubleshoot another problem. A stiffness took over his neck and shoulders, and his jaw muscles flexed unconsciously. He tried slowing down his breathing and stroking his goatee, but neither helped him relax much. He had a hard time pushing out the mental picture of his boss growing fat on his comfy couch, watching SportsCenter in his lavish home theater and then calling it an early night.

So, so wrong, he kept thinking. He barely kept himself from muttering a curse under his breath when he heard a voice from the doorway into his office.

"You alright, boss?"

Stephen suddenly sat upright on his seat, eyes wide with embarrassment. He looked up to see Jared's head poking in through the doorway. It only took a quick moment for him to recompose himself as he leaned his tall, slim frame back into his tilting chair. He let out a long sigh. Even though it was already 6:30 on a Thursday night, Jared's smile was still infectious. Stephen grinned back and shook his head.

"Sorry, man. Airspace Shipping just called and said that their manifest screens went blank a half hour ago. Package signals aren't syncing up. I don't think it's a transmission problem: only a few'd go blank. But since they all did, either the receivers went down or the code crashed. The bad news is that we gotta figure this out right away. Could be a late night." He ran his fingers through his hair as he let out another sigh.

Jared came around Stephen's desk and immediately began poring over Stephen's computer screen. Jared was proof that the dress code at Mobiship was lenient: a T-shirt, cargo shorts and sandals. On his left arm, he had a tattoo of three horizontal bars that reminded Stephen of military stripes.

As he studied the code, Jared asked with a knowing grin, "The big guy cut out again?"

"Yeah," Stephen said, exhaling strongly.

"Don't let it get to you, dude," Jared said, jabbing him in the shoulder hard enough to make him wince. "We'll get this done quicker than you think."

STAR

Jared was right. The blips on the screen came back to life just before eleven.

He had been hired at Mobiship Technologies right out of college, just a couple of months earlier. But Mobiship was lucky to nab him. As a gifted coder from UCLA, he had his pick of firms in Silicon Valley and Seattle. But a couple of spring breaks in "America's Finest City" had convinced him to seek San Diego's endless summer and sugar-sand beaches. If Stephen had concerns about Jared's youthfulness, he wasn't worried about his talent. In short time, Jared was regarded as Mobiship's star programmer, and Stephen circled around him like a mother eagle, keeping other teams from snatching his hatchling away.

On this particular night, Stephen's hunch was dead on: the problem was in the code, which had been written before Jared's arrival. Under the perfect storm of circumstances, it had been known to lock up before. Even so, Jared was able to isolate the problem and have it fixed in a few hours. Stephen gave his team parting fist bumps, thanked Jared in front of the team and left the office.

He did not have to take the freeway to get home, not that it mattered at this time of night. All he had to do was cross the 15 from his Rancho Bernardo office to Poway. In ten minutes, he would be in the arms of his wife, Misun. But Luke and Brandon would already be sleeping, and he felt a pang of guilt. His four-year-old and two-year-old weren't getting much face time lately, and they weren't getting any younger. Neither was he.

Stephen pulled up to a red light. In the quiet of his hybrid engine, his thoughts turned back to work. He let a question rise to his mind, one that would haunt him again and again.

Is this what I'm supposed to do with my life?

He let out yet another long sigh. But this time, he was too tired to even try for a coherent answer, so he let his mind-numbed autopilot take him home.

Thank God tomorrow's Friday, he thought as he unlocked his front door. Only one more routine day to make it to the weekend. But Friday would be anything but routine.

RHYTHM

Stephen took his seat in the cafeteria while others started to trickle in for lunch. As he started to open his meal, he heard sandals slapping loudly on the floor. He looked up to see Jared bounding fast toward him from the cashier's line. He plopped down hard at Stephen's table, eyes bulging, barely able to speak from the surging excitement. Stephen looked down and started to fiddle awkwardly with his lunch bag.

"I knew it, I knew it!" Jared almost yelled.

Stephen looked up at him, without a clue to what he was talking about.

"You're a *Christian,* aren't you!" Jared asked repeatedly, too excited to be cautious. "I saw you praying for your lunch!"

Stephen noticed that others were turning their heads to see the growing spectacle, so he tried to hush Jared with his gesturing hands. He didn't need others to make assumptions about him at the office, especially given common opinions about Christians these days. He nodded quickly to Jared as he whispered, "Yeah. Why do you ask?"

Jared jumped out of his chair, almost knocking it over. He clapped his hands loudly as he hopped around the table and bent down to give him a huge hug. Stephen unconsciously squirmed, feeling the stares in the cafeteria boring down on him. Jared grabbed him by the shoulders, stared straight into his eyes and said triumphantly: "Dude! This is a God-setup!" He started throwing his fists in the air, like he was celebrating a touchdown. Stephen found his lack of self-restraint unnerving.

After Stephen finally coaxed him to sit down, Jared said, "Sorry, I get a little carried away sometimes."

"Really?" said Stephen with a glare.

Jared then explained with less volume that he had become a Christian about eight months ago. He'd been praying for an older mentor at his new job so that he could learn how to be a faithful Christian at work. If Stephen was surprised by the first expressions of jubilation, he certainly wasn't prepared for the next question.

"So, when are we going to get started?"

Stephen paused a bit, trying to understand the request. "Started with what?"

"Discipling me, of course!" His arms were wide open, and Stephen feared another bear hug coming his direction. He unconsciously kicked his seat back a bit. He'd never discipled anyone before—at least not since college, and that was a long time ago.

"Um, what would that look like?" asked Stephen.

"I thought you would know. I was told to go find a discipler when I got to my new workplace. And here you are!" He pointed at him repeatedly with both hands and a huge smile, with enough verve to poke him all the way through.

Stephen didn't know what to say at that point, but he also didn't want to crush the first flush of a new believer's spiritual life. So he answered casually, not knowing what he was about to get into.

"Okay. How about lunch next week? Tuesday. We can talk about what it looks like then."

"Right on," Jared said as he got up and came around the table to jab him in the arm. "Tuesdays it is."

ODDS

Stephen tried to ignore the fact that Jared added an "s" at the end of *Tuesday*, but he didn't have the heart to correct him. So they met week after week. With each passing week, he knew that he was *supposed* to help him grow in faith. But he couldn't shake the feeling that he had no idea what he was doing.

"So how do I *know*?" asked Jared on their third meeting. "How would I know if Jackie's the one?"

Stephen stared down at his turkey sandwich and his thoughts screamed at him: *He's seriously asking me about the one? How should I know? Shouldn't we be talking about something else, like how his devotional times are going?*

He looked around the cafeteria for some sort of inspiration. It looked like the aftermath of Ikea invading an Asian-inspired frozen yogurt shop. Round white tables and white plastic dining chairs with orange seat cushions occupied most of the space in the cafeteria. The floors were made up of large and shiny rectangular tiles in a dark, speckly gray. But the smells of chicken soup, turkey paninis and French fries that wafted over from the kitchen felt out of place. Clearly, the interior decorator and the cook didn't talk to each other.

Nothing.

"I don't know," said Stephen. He wasn't trying that hard, wanting to move on to more spiritual topics.

"What do you mean you don't know?" Jared asked, with eyes widening in frustration.

Stephen stared across at Jared, who still waited for an answer. His mind wandered a bit, trying to figure out where Jared was from. Jared was a darker shade of tan. Perhaps he was Latino. His eyes felt like they had a hint of Asian in them, but also seemed too round for that. He had dark, curly hair, but it looked too wavy to be of African descent. He was also a little shorter than average and of a stocky build, but that didn't give him any more clues. Nothing lined up neatly. And he didn't have the guts to ask point-blank. As his supervisor, he didn't want to ask Jared anything that might slap him with a lawsuit.

"Shouldn't we be talking about something else?" asked Stephen bluntly, after he noticed the longer silence.

"But dude, isn't this important to my spiritual life?" he said with some urgency.

Stephen had mentored a handful of people at work, particularly as a project manager. He helped them get more proficient at their jobs. But that's so much clearer. He provided skill training and clear expectations. Spiritual mentoring, in contrast, felt vague.

He thought back to college and wondered how effective his efforts at discipling had been. Of the twelve people in the small group he had led, five no longer followed Jesus. One rejected the faith to marry his husband in New York. He probably would've said that the faith rejected him. Another stopped going to church altogether after she lost her husband in a freak camping accident. A third just faded, never finding a church she could call home after college; after bouncing from this community to that, she finally decided that church didn't have much to offer her. A fourth got really busy with his life as a lawyer, started dating someone who was skeptical toward anything religious and didn't darken the doorway of a church ever again.

Others still went to church, but when he talked with them he could've been hanging out with anyone. Nothing stood out about their lives.

Only Stephanie seemed faithful and vibrant. She became a Christian in his small group and enjoyed being a professor of philosophy back on the East Coast. His soul found life talking with her: she talked about God in ways that made him feel real and close.

One out of twelve. No one would invest on those odds.

SUSHI

That evening, Stephen had to stay a little later at work. Again. But when he was able to peel away just before seven, he raced home. When he walked in through the garage door, he hugged his parents who had already come down from Mission Viejo, and he offered many thanks. Then he looked up the staircase just in time to catch his wife coming down in a black cocktail dress.

Flirtatiously, he let his jaw go slack. Misun flipped her straight black hair knowingly and flashed a smile. She was ready for their first date in months, and after a quick kiss he rushed upstairs to grab a dark gray jacket.

They made it on time for their reservation at Poway's new sushi restaurant. The dining area was cavernous, decorated with the requisite faux-Asian artifacts hanging on the walls. And though the many Japanese fountains bubbled over with Zen-like regularity, the trance music overpowered any sense of peace and reminded them to be as hip as the restaurant tried to be.

If Stephen and Misun felt a little out of place, they didn't look it. They placed themselves in the chef's hands, and each dish that came out topped the previous one. Neither one dared to let the yellowtail sashimi with sisho-infused miso sauce and balsamic vinegar or the kunamoto oyster topped with uni and caviar be soiled by soy sauce. Every bite had been perfected and didn't need any embellishment.

"Nice to get out of the house, right?" said Stephen, grinning.

He unconsciously bobbed his head up and down with the music: *un-ce, un-ce, un-ce, un-ce* . . .

Misun smiled back and nodded while savoring her last bite. Then she leaned in, "So, how are you doing these days?" She was thankful for an adult conversation.

"I'm having fun thinking about the past these days. Remember when your parents used to call me 'Mr. Bah-nah-nah'?"

She laughed. "Yeah. They couldn't pronounce Cavanaugh, so they called you Mr. Banana instead. You did good to win them over. I know lots of Korean parents who wouldn't have budged."

"Well, here's to eleven years!" he said, as he lifted his drink.

"Eleven years," she smiled back.

After taking another mouthful of bluefin sashimi with truffles, Stephen said, "Let me ask *you* something. Would you support me in *anything* I wanted to do?"

"Of course," she said lightly.

"Well, what if I'm not doing what I'm supposed to be doing? I'm thirty-eight, and I thought I'd be doing something different by now."

"Like what?" she said, as her hand reached out for the spicy tuna on crispy rice.

"I don't know. Maybe full-time ministry?"

She almost choked on her tuna, thinking that he was joking. She sobered up quickly: "Oh, you're being serious. Sorry, honey. Okay, I'm all ears. Why do you want to be in ministry?"

"I know I'm not *supposed* to think this, but if we were *really* faithful to Jesus, wouldn't we all go into full-time ministry?"

"You know what I say after Pastor Rob's sermons. Imagine me saying that to you *every* week," she joked.

He laughed and nodded. Then, he wistfully looked out over

her shoulder at nothing in particular and said, "I just think I was made for something more than this. I'm coming home later and later. And for what? It's just a paycheck . . ."

She reached across the table and placed her hand on his arm. "It's a helpful paycheck. We've got two kids and a mortgage to pay, and I'm not working yet. Give it a few years, when the kids go to school and when I'm working, and then we can figure something out."

"I know, I know," he sighed. "I'm not planning to quit. I guess I'm just not that happy. I want to feel alive. Or feel *something.* I just don't know what I'm supposed to be doing, but I'm pretty sure I'm not doing it."

Misun fought her temptation to put a few possible options forward and instead gripped his forearm reassuringly. "I just want you to know that I get it. I *un-der-stand.*" She said the last word slowly and with a mischievous smile, poking a little fun at his need for validation.

He grinned back and let his shoulders relax. He knew it was a practiced line but still appreciated it.

"I promise not to do anything drastic," he offered.

She thought for a moment, then suddenly brightened up with a huge smile, "Come on. Keep eating. You'll feel better."

And he did. The food was amazing, and he even had fun when Misun forced him onto the dance floor. She was the better dancer, and he, well, did his best with what God gave him. As the house beat thumped louder and louder, there wasn't much room left to think about the future or his calling.

TEA

Stephen and Misun walked through the garage door after one o'clock in the morning, knowing that his parents and the kids would be fast asleep. They giggled arm-in-arm and tiptoed upstairs to the bedroom.

Misun was soon fast asleep, but Stephen had trouble finding slumber that night. He had tossed and turned for about an hour and then gave up. He went downstairs to make some tea, thinking that it would help him get to sleep.

He sat down at the kitchen table with his steaming cup of chamomile tea and looked around. The dimmed recessed lights allowed him to see his spacious kitchen with its granite countertops and stainless steel appliances. When he looked past the sink, he could see his family room, with a large flat-screen television hanging off the wall. The speakers were built into the ceiling and the walls and could carry some serious sound. A tinge of guilt crept in.

He couldn't shake the sense that he was living out someone else's dream. Engineering gave him a salary that allowed him to live well without financial worries, especially now that he was a project manager at the firm. He had a beautiful wife, two healthy kids and good enough credit to live in a decent suburb. He lived close to work and church, and his kids would end up in great schools once they were old enough. Sure, there was nothing particularly wrong with having all of this stuff, but he also felt *too* comfortable. Is this what it means to live in the kingdom?

He could've chosen a life that was, in his mind, more devout. He thought back to a conversation that he had with his campus minister many years ago. *Maybe I should've gone on staff,* thought Stephen. It was his call to make: his parents were supportive either way. But he didn't get a call from heaven. No dew on the fleece. No flash of lightning from the sky. So he made a practical decision.

I could always go back to ministry, he thought then.

But sixteen years later, he was still at the firm. And now he had a family to support. His salary had grown, so much so that it was painful just thinking about a pay cut to be in full-time ministry.

And seminary? At my age?

Yet he couldn't help but think that maybe his faith would look different today if he had said yes to his staff worker all those years ago.

Sure, he was an elder in the church, one of the youngest ones in the church's history. He was generous and gave to various nonprofits. But he always felt pressed for time, and, more and more lately, his family and church were getting less of it.

What is my faith supposed to look like today?

In college, he felt like his faith was on fire. Now he wondered if his faith had any heat—that his neighbors or the community around him could feel—at all.

BALL

Bleary-eyed, Stephen reclined in his office chair. He already had two cups of coffee this Monday morning, and after answering some emails and planning out his week, his mind groped about for direction. If he didn't have answers about his own life, he surely didn't have any for Jared's.

He repeatedly shot a paper ball into the air, sighing. Four meetings with Jared had come and gone. Though Jared was still excited and eager, Stephen continued to have no idea how to channel that energy into something more productive. He couldn't honestly think of anything more to recommend him. He had learned that Jared read his Bible every day. He prayed each morning. He went to church each weekend and had joined a young adult small group.

What else was he supposed to do? What else am I supposed to teach him?

Stephen, always prone to enjoy any fantasy about leaving Mobiship, let himself be tempted with the thought of going to seminary: *If I went, then maybe I would be able to help him.*

But there were other things that Stephen was worried about. Jared was always thinking about the ladies: who he liked, who he was interested in, who he was dating. It came up in every conversation. He'd only been in town for three months, and already he seemed to have been on nine or ten dates. Stephen couldn't keep count.

Even if Jared wasn't girl-crazy, what else would he teach him? Jared knew the basics: he knew that his sins were forgiven through Jesus' death on the cross. Now what? Just remember what was done for him? Should he learn more of the Bible? All of it? It's a long book. Is it important for Jared to master every little detail? If not, what's the most important? The stuff in red letters? The Epistles? Or should he teach some sort of systematic theology, or go through other Christian books? Stephen himself certainly was no master of biblical details, though he also gained a lot from the thirty-plus years of his own church upbringing. But Jared didn't grow up in the church and really had a short time at his campus fellowship as well. So his familiarity with the Scriptures was comparatively low. Getting him up to speed seemed like a seminary professor's job or, at least, a pastor's job. Not his.

I know I'm supposed to help him become like Jesus, he reassured himself as he continued to toss his paper ball into the air. But what does that mean? How would Jesus be and act today? Back in Jesus' day, the number of occupations seemed so much more limited. There weren't any computer programmers or electrical engineers then, right? *Would Jesus be an engineer?* He was, after all, a construction worker by trade. But it does take a lot of training to do today's highly specialized professions: Would Jesus approve of the time spent? The firm also helps track the delivery of weapons. Is it okay to work here? Would Jesus contribute to the rampant militarism in our country? Or the materialism, for that matter? It's simple, though not easy, to be like Jesus if we narrow it down to the fruit of the Spirit in our personal character, but aren't we also supposed to love our neighbors and seek justice?

He took a shot at a wastepaper basket across the room. He missed badly, and the paper ball rolled out into the hallway. He rubbed his face in his hands as he got up to get it.

Yet another miss . . .

HELP

Stephen bent over to pick up the paper ball, and when he stood back up, he felt the pain of a familiar greeting. He began to rub his shoulder while Jared grinned.

"What's going on?" he asked. They caught up about the weekend. Stephen mentioned his date, and Jared talked about *both* of his.

"But I don't think either of them are going to work out," Jared said.

"Okay, let's talk more about them on Tuesday," said Stephen, although he felt a twinge of regret immediately after the words left his mouth.

He went back into his office, sank back into his chair and rolled forward to his computer screen. Online, he searched: *discipleship*. He ordered a few discipleship books that came up that were highly rated and seemed relevant. Then he opened his email client and finally sent off a desperate message to a friend at church.

To: bridge@campusministries.org
Subject: help!

IDEA

Dinner was over and the grown-ups mingled freely in the vast living room. Just beyond the floor-to-ceiling windows, tiny waves lapped in a large, lighted swimming pool.

Stephen and Misun never got used to the approach to this house. From the front gate, the Taylors' neighbors were unseen, even though it was a residential neighborhood just north of San Diego. When the buzzer sounded to let people in, the gate swung open to reveal a tree-lined, dirt driveway with a lagoon flowing into the Pacific on their left and a large pond on their right. The house was still out of sight. After a while, the driveway turned up into a cul-de-sac toward a large mission-style home, with curved, dirt-red adobe tiles for the roof. It felt like a resort, which was no accident. The Taylors amassed their wealth on a chain of high-end resorts that dotted the California coast, recently expanding into Phoenix, Las Vegas and Hawaii.

Every once in a while, the Taylors would invite their friends over from church for a dinner and hangout. Eighteen adults and their children trekked over on this Friday evening, taking advantage of the free babysitting offered by one of the Taylor daughters.

Stephen looked around and wondered for a moment: *What would I do with all this? Would I have the courage to start giving it away as they have?*

"I haven't said hi to you guys yet," Bridget said with a huge smile, interrupting his thoughts. She hugged them both.

"Bridge, I don't know how you manage to look so good," Misun said. Everyone called her Bridge.

"Are you kidding? Look at *you!* " she replied, as her brown eyes looked admiringly through her hip black glasses. Bridge was quite stylish: she wore a dark blue patterned scarf over her white flowing blouse and dark jeans, and her salt-and-pepper hair was clipped short around her round face. For someone in her mid-fifties, she exuded youthful energy. It was probably the fruit of serving as a campus minister at the University of California, San Diego, over the past thirty years.

Every Thursday night, over four hundred students gathered to worship where she served. She had been given many chances to rise up in the organizational ranks, to serve as a director over larger swaths of ministry. But she'd known by the time she was in her thirties that she would never leave direct ministry to college students. She wanted to be as close to them as possible, and moving up the ladder felt more like a curse than a promotion.

"Did you get my email?" Stephen asked.

"Yes, I did. Sorry, we had a large group last night, and every week it gets really busy right up to it. But it was *epic.*" That felt natural coming out of her mouth, in a way that few people her age could've pulled off.

"What happened? How did the fellowship respond to the stuff happening on campus?"

"There's so much to tell, so I'll update you soon," she said. Stephen and Misun financially and prayerfully supported her ministry and received her email updates. "I'm still processing what happened. But why did you want to meet up?"

"I wanted to pick your brain about something. This guy at work asked me to disciple him—a new believer who just graduated from college. But I have no idea what I'm doing. I was wondering if you could help me."

"Sure! It's a huge question, eh? What would you like to know?"

"I repeat," he said in a robotic monotone, "I have no idea what I'm doing."

"Gotcha," she said with a smile. "Have you ever discipled anyone before?"

"Not *really*. Plus, these young guys seem really different these days."

BOOMERS

Bridge pointed over to a corner of the immense living room, where a couple of plush leather chairs and a lamp on a round, dark-brown side table beckoned them to come and sit. Most of the furniture in the Taylors' home were leftovers from their resorts.

"Is this okay?" Stephen asked Misun.

"Sure," said Misun. "Bridge, I'll talk to you later." She joined another group near the middle of the room and, within a moment, was already laughing with the others.

Stephen and Bridge slumped down into the cozy chairs.

"So, you think the young folks are different than we were, eh?" Bridge asked, the last word betraying her Vancouver roots.

"We?" said Stephen, flashing a grin.

"Ouch!" she said, hands up in mock surrender. "Not right to tease your *jie jie!*" Stephen knew that the last two words meant *big sister* in Mandarin, since she said it often. "These young folks *are* different. I've been in ministry a long time. I've ministered to some Baby Boomers, but mostly Generation Xers and Millennials. I just gave a seminar on this, so it's fresh in my mind. Want to hear about the differences?"

"Absolutely." Stephen leaned in to hear her over the conversation in the room. Bridge settled into her chair and looked up in thought. She waited for a dramatic moment out of a teacher's habit.

"There's an old Arab proverb that says, 'Men resemble the times more than they resemble their fathers.' *When* we were born seems to shape us in some powerful way. Each generation has its own vibe and feel, struggling with its own sense of meaning and purpose. I call it 'the spiritual question of the day.' Does that make sense?" She saw him nod, but her teaching instincts kicked in.

"Hold on," she said. She reached down into her bag and pulled out a leather folio. She opened it, and it revealed a standard lined notepad and an inner loop that held a pen.

"Do you always pull that out?" he joked.

"I can still be old school in some things. Plus, it's always good to be clear, eh?" she said. She turned the folio sideways and then wrote at the top of the page: *the spiritual question of the day.*

"Let's start with my generation," she continued. "The Baby Boomers were born roughly between 1943 and 1960. They got their name because of the huge uptick in babies born—the baby boom—to GIs after they returned from World War II." As she said this, she wrote: *Boomers (b. 1943-1960).*

"Where do those dates come from?"

"Census data. The dates mark the bulges in population data, give or take a year or two. The dates aren't that important, though: if you're a few years off—or many, for that matter—you may still relate to a different generation. For our purposes, it's more about a mindset than exactly when you were born. We're talking about generalities here, so of course not everyone fits into the generation they're assigned."

Her voice was strong and confident. She looked Stephen in the eye and made sure that he was keeping track.

"We're about sixty to eighty million, depending on who's counting," she said. "We're in our fifties and sixties now, as you so *dared* to remind me." She gave him an accusing glare. He laughed.

"We were brought up in a *modern* worldview," she continued. "Absolute truth exists and is something to be found. We should seek it, live by it, make decisions through it, change our lives guided by it. So our spiritual question was, 'What is true?'" She then wrote the question in her chart, underlining the final word:

Spiritual Question of the Day

Boomers
(b. 1943-1960)   *What is true?*

Stephen had often heard older people talk about how the youth are losing their knowledge of the truth. In Christian circles, that usually meant the Bible.

"The pursuit of truth was king," she continued. "Whether it was in science, religion, philosophy, art or culture at large, they looked for what was *true*. Rationality, logic, evidence, knowledge were *the* sources of authority. If you could prove it, then it was true. If it was true, then it was meant to guide our lives. But if you couldn't, then it was deemed false."

Stephen was tracking, and he couldn't help but think how alienating this worldview was to him. *Truth? Really? That's all they wanted? How would you even know what's true? How could we ever tease out our own biases?* Still, he was listening and just nodded.

"To answer this question for unbelievers, you had to prove that the Christian faith was based on facts or logic that were undeniable—or at least reasonable. Prove that the Bible is legitimate history and prove authorship, dates, the accuracy of the copies. You get the gist. Prove that Jesus actually walked on the planet, flesh and all. Prove that he actually died on the cross. Prove that he rose again. Because if you could, then you would be heard. Someone might choose Christianity because you could prove it to be true. And the assumption was, when someone saw that it was true, they would reorient their lives around that very fact—because it was *true!* It had huge implications: if faith was about passing along the knowledge of the faith, the most efficient way to do that was in large auditoriums. The megachurch, eh? And of course, you'd push for decisions: if people made a decision to follow Jesus, based on the truth, then everything else in the post-decision Christian should fall into place. But the post-decision life doesn't seem to work out that way these days, does it?"

Stephen always hated the push toward decisions. It felt manipulative. But now he could see why it might have been effective, at least for previous generations. He was about to ask, *What would work for people today?* But she said, as if she were reading his mind, "But the next generation—your generation—came along, and you all were really different."

XERS

Misun had moved on to another couple in the corner and when he looked up their eyes met.

He raised his eyebrows and nodded, which translated into a real language between spouses: *Is this okay that I'm still talking, or did you want to leave?*

She smiled and nodded back: *Sure, I'm still good and talking with friends. If you want to stay longer, that's fine with me—I'm not in a hurry.* Then she gave him a thumbs-up: *And we've got free babysitting!*

He smiled, *Thanks!* Then he turned his attention back to Bridge, who didn't miss the nonverbals either.

"Generation X," Bridge said, "was born roughly between 1961-1981, and are about forty to sixty million, which makes them smaller than the generations they're sandwiched in between. That's why others call your generation Busters: the baby *bust* after the baby boom." She continued to fill out the chart.

"What makes them really unique is that they're the first truly postmodern generation. There are always differences between generations, but worldview shifts take longer, often up to five hundred years or so. It's huge! And one major shift in worldview is that they didn't believe in absolute truth anymore. Like Pilate, they asked, 'What is truth?' They didn't trust it. They saw that 'truth' was often used to crush the voice of the other, often as a tool of oppression."

"How did that happen?" he asked.

"The pursuit of truth, particularly through science, did not produce the promised utopia. Instead, the world was plunged into a larger scale of violence through two world wars. The world didn't get better, and people started to get disillusioned. In addition, people used 'science' to claim that they were genetically superior to other ethnicities and cultures, and science gave racism the reasons it needed to put people into servitude or slaughter them outright, like in Nazi Germany. The pursuit of truth was often bent for oppressive means. It wasn't trustworthy anymore.

"Xers, in particular, grew up skeptical about anything that self-proclaims that it is true. How could we know if it is true or not, since we all come with inherent biases? No one and nothing could be trusted, because everyone has an agenda. Anything that smelled of institutionalism, big budget, marketing or a program was viewed with suspicion. Everyone must be spinning for their own ends. Xers are the best BS detectors on the planet."

Stephen laughed out loud on that one. At first, the description of Xers sounded really jaded, but he knew it was fair. He hated it when people spun things positively all the time, especially when he could see that something else was up. People should, he thought, drop their masks and just be themselves.

"In one sense, it's easy to see why Xers are so skeptical. They were the most aborted generation in history. If they made it out alive, they often had only one parent, as divorce spiked with the Boomers. If they had both parents, then they probably both worked, creating a generation of latchkey kids: children who came home to an empty house. They felt that Boomers lived for themselves, and Xers were left high and dry in a time that felt scarier with each passing day. Culture shifted from a G-rated to an

R-rated world, and they lived under the threat of nuclear war, AIDS and an economy that dipped when they graduated from college. No wonder they didn't trust other generations, since they had messed up the world around them. So Xers learned to survive on their own."

"That sounds like me," he said, feeling a little exposed. "But I don't like being clumped with others. I don't think it's true for everyone."

"You're such an Xer," she teased. "Don't want to be labeled, eh? Well, it's the Xers' posture of distrust that put you at odds with the Boomers. They wanted to hand down their organizations and institutions to your generation, but you didn't want them. They felt oppressive to you as you sought something more authentic. In that rejection, they thought you all were a bunch of slackers. That's where your name comes from: Generation X. It was first used for another generation, to describe their lack of identity in the face of an uncertain future. But it was placed on your generation, because Boomers thought you were lost.

"But you're not. You're prophets and innovators. Your generation came up with the dot-coms. Christian Xers question the tried-and-true theology of the Boomers. It's what they do. They don't even like the Boomers' starting question, remember— *What is true?* But Boomers think you're undermining the truth with your questions. That's why we don't like you very much, and vice versa."

She nailed him. He often took what older people said with a grain of salt, especially if he thought they had a particular agenda.

"Now, I'm just talking in generalities. *I* still like you," she winked. "So, your generation's spiritual question is very different. You didn't care about the same *kind* of truth. If the spiritual question of the Boomers was 'What is true?' then the question for the Xers is 'What is real?'" She wrote the question out on the notepad:

Spiritual Question of the Day

Boomers
(b. 1943-1960)   *what is true?*

Generation X
(b. 1961-1981)   *what is real?*

"That makes a lot of sense. When you were describing the Boomers' question, I kept thinking about how that didn't make any sense at all. But if someone is real and authentic, I'd listen."

"Exactly. Your generation wanted to know that faith wasn't something you memorized or argued about, but something *real* and lived out. You wanted to see and experience a faith that was genuine. And if it was real for someone else, then it could be real for you. So when Christian Xers started reaching out to their peers, they had to put away the arguments. I remember when we hosted a campus outreach and brought in one of our best apologists of the day, and it bombed. He was so condescending that he didn't endear himself to anyone, though he was intellectually right. He just seemed like a jerk, and the ones asking questions seemed more thoughtful, caring, understanding. We had to shift if we wanted to remain relevant to your generation."

Stephen remembered those days. Now he was seeing why those approaches weren't working anymore. He wished he had heard this when he was in college. Perhaps he would've saved his fellowship from those painfully awkward outreach events.

"So instead, if we wanted to introduce people to Jesus, we needed to do things differently. We might have an event where a speaker would be open about their messed-up past, and even the stuff they were struggling with now, and show how Jesus was meeting them. Drop the masks. Kill the spin. It was just about being as raw as possible to build trust and then to share an authentic story of how Jesus was transforming us. Powerful, eh? And then we invited others to experience the same thing. Through this, curiosity sparked. With this generation, reason and science lost its authority, while experience and community gained theirs."

"Makes sense," he said.

"When Xers were on campus, I spent lots of time in coffee shops, just trying to convince people that I was trustworthy enough to allow me to speak into their lives. Distrust, remember? But when the Millennials came to town," she said while waving her hands, "I couldn't shoo them away."

MILLENNIALS

Stephen felt some regret as he realized that he hadn't sought Bridge for counsel before. Even though he supported her ministry, he hadn't thought to go to her with these kinds of questions. But Bridge clearly knew her stuff, and he could sense that he'd soon have a better idea of what to do with Jared.

Bridge wrote out the name and dates of the next generation on her notepad and said, "The Millennials were born from 1982 to 2002. They're bigger than either of the previous generations: around eighty to one hundred million strong. They got their name because they were born at the turn of the millennium. Not very original, eh? I guess it's better than other names. Some call them *Gen Y* because they're born after Gen X. That's not going to stick: *they* won't want to be named as a sequel. Others call them Mosaics, because of their idiosyncratic and eclectic tastes. Neither's great."

"Neither is Generation X," he said flatly.

She laughed. "But you didn't put up a fight, eh? Like Xers, they're also a postmodern generation, where absolute truth is still on the ropes. But they're also very different than Xers. Some Christian Xer leaders make no distinctions between the two, clumping them both under terms like *emerging* or *postmodern* generations. They predicted that Millennials would be repelled by big churches or huge productions. But they're way off. They don't seem to mind going big. They conform much more easily than you guys did."

"That makes sense. I've seen these guys stick brand logos on their backpacks and computers. Not many Xers would do that, unless you were doing it for work."

"Yes, they don't have the revulsion to marketing that your generation did. They've been marketed to all their lives. They like it: 'Personalized attention for me? Perfect.'" She gave a thumbs-up as she said the last word.

Stephen hoped he would like this generation by the time Bridge was done.

"If Xers felt neglected, Millennials grew up sheltered," she continued. "With Xers and young Boomers reacting to the latchkey phenomenon, they created idyllic environments for their children to make them feel special. Where Xers felt criticized, Millennials were encouraged and praised. They were the center of their homes. But it gets stressful taking care of the kids all the time, eh?"

"Ain't that the truth," said Stephen. The bags under his eyes reminded him of the demands of young parenthood. "I don't remember booster seats in cars, just a seatbelt. I walked to school on my own when I was five. And when did we start giving out party favors for birthday parties? Only guests used to bring gifts. We're all about the kids these days, and it's crazy!" He paused, then added, "But I also want to make sure my own kids are okay too!" He motioned the pulling out of his own hair.

"Torn, eh?" she winked. "You just want to make sure that your kids get every chance they need. But in a way, you're also a generation that's most afraid of your children. You don't want to mess them up with some trauma that messed you guys up. So you work extra hard to make sure they have everything they'll ever need. But you're actually raising the generation after the Millennials, and if generational theory holds up, you'll smother your children even more. But the parents of Millennials were still more protective than your parents. *Helicopter parents,* right? I can't remember a time in my thirty years on campus when I talked to parents more! So Millennials got used to the involvement of older people. Unlike Xers, they like it. They *crave* it. Plus, modern life overloads them with a great deal of choice: they'd rather have an expert tell them what to do than think through it for themselves."

"That's why!" Stephen exclaimed, almost slapping his own forehead. "Jared came to me, so ready. He asked lots of questions when he first started working for us. But he also followed the direction of his campus minister and immediately sought me as a mentor. He seemed way too eager, more than I was at his age, at least."

"Hold on, let me read something," she said, as she reached into her bag and got out her cell phone to pull up a document from her cloud storage. She pulled on some reading glasses and started to read:

"'Millennials can heed moral exemplars, and respond to principled leaders, far better than most of today's adults could when young. That's the opportunity side. Yet these new youths might decisively oppose nominal leaders who fail to provide real direction, and they might be inclined to support misguided leaders if better alternatives aren't available. That's the danger side.'"

"If you had a tablet, you might not need those glasses," he joked.

"Take it easy, eh?" she smiled. "I've got my phone and my *paper* pad. Don't need the other stuff! But that's what we're up against. These guys will follow a great vision and a great plan, but they don't always have the skills to follow through on those plans. You Xers learned how to survive because you had to. You learned some life skills, like doing the laundry and balancing your budget. These guys, however, were coddled. It was like they were a cocoon prematurely opened to help out the caterpillar, but in so doing the butterfly never gained the strength to fly. In the same way, the Millennials often didn't learn the necessary life skills to make it as adults and often just leaned on their parents to do it for them."

Stephen thought about Jared. He just thought everyone felt younger as he got older. But now, he had good reason to think that they were also comparatively more immature, even for their age. He thought about Jared. He could do so much. But he always asked for advice, almost unsure of what to do next, except when it came to actual coding. He was idealistic and hopeful, and yet he didn't seem like he had a plan.

"Along the way, they're hyper-empowered by affordable, yet powerful, technology. Nowadays, your cell phone is obsolete if you don't have a video camera, a music player and web access built in, so anyone can find their fifteen minutes of fame, or infamy, in an upload. It can fuel a bit of narcissism, eh? They are connected like no other generation. So they can do a great amount of good, but one slip and their drunken images will be plastered online. They need guidance but are also more willing to receive it."

Stephen nodded. He had wondered why people would put self-incriminating photos of themselves out for the world to see. It definitely didn't help their future careers.

"The upside for Millennials is that they're achievers. You Xers wanted work-life balance. These guys want to get something done. Maybe the Boomer in me likes that," she said with a wink. "If the Xers were trying to survive and challenge the status quo, Millennials want to know the cultural game and win it. I remember a journalist saying, 'Millennials will definitely not want to be known as Gen Y. Generation A+, though—that might be a different story.'"

Stephen unconsciously snorted. "That just sounds stressful," he joked.

"It is," she said in all seriousness. "And they often are. But they also have an optimistic, can-do spirit. They really think they can accomplish some good. They want to get involved. They really think that if everyone works together, they can change the world. Couple this with their narcissism, and Bono becomes their patron saint: he's rich and famous, but still does a great deal of good in the world. He's the perfect fit for this generation."

"That can lead to some serious problems, no? Not everyone can be a rock star. Not everyone should even try."

"True," she laughed. "And they often have big dreams, but don't have a day-by-day plan to get there. But from this, do you get a sense of what their spiritual question might be? If the spiritual question for Boomers is 'What is true?' and for the Xers, 'What is real?' then what's the spiritual question of the day for Millennials?"

She let the question hang in the air for a moment, then wrote it down:

Spiritual Question of the Day

Boomers (b. 1943–1960)	what is <u>true</u>?
Generation X (b. 1961–1981)	what is <u>real</u>?
Millennials (b. 1982–2002)	what is <u>good</u>?

"Makes sense, right? They want to know if the Christian faith is actually good for the world," she continued. "The Internet has enabled them to be acutely aware of the rest of the world, and so they're exposed—at least virtually—to global poverty, the AIDS pandemic, human trafficking, immigration issues, conflict zones and the systems of injustice and oppression and greed. The 1 percent, eh? And they want to know if the Christian faith has an answer to the problems they see in the world today. That question hangs in the air of the times. If we would just be less extreme in our religious beliefs and practices, then we wouldn't have the global and community violence that abound today, right? Everyone should just chill out about religion, because it divides us. Religion, to many of them, is the problem."

"I hear that a lot," said Stephen. "Even from older people." To him, the voices in the media had gotten more hostile toward the Christian faith. The '90s felt far more open to spirituality. These days, he felt like he had to defend his faith from unfair stereotypes.

"The Millennials' question has bled into wider culture: Is Christianity any good for the world? Many movies, TV shows, and even opinion-shapers wonder if our world would be better without religious extremists. You hear the question echoed in bestselling books like *God Is Not Great* or *The God Delusion*. Even video games hijack religious language for their villains. If we can't answer that question—What good does the Christian faith bring?—skeptics will block their ears to us. Our credibility will drop to nothing, and we'll be shoved off to the margins. Now, being on the margins isn't always a bad thing, but I wonder if we're actually following the words of Jesus if we don't have anything to offer that is good in *this* world and not just in the world to come."

¡GENS?

Bridge stopped for a second, almost to see how Stephen would respond. She was on a roll, and this kind of talk stuck with students, but she didn't really know where Stephen was on a theological or political scale. Wondering if she had overstepped her bounds, she asked, "What do you think about that?"

Stephen wasn't checking up on Misun anymore and didn't notice that she was making her way toward them. He looked down, deep in thought. "That last statement was strong, but," he said hesitatingly, "I agree with most of it. There has to be something about faith that is also on this side of eternity. I just haven't heard anyone say it that strongly."

All of this had major implications for how to share and live out the Christian faith. Stephen wondered how all of this would affect his children, and so he asked: "What about my kids' generation?"

"Well, that's hard to predict," Bridge said. "The next generation aren't even teens yet, having been born, at the earliest, in 2003. We don't even know what to call them, whether they are the *Internet Generation, the New Silents,* or *Generation Z,* just to name a few."

"Gen Z isn't going to cut it."

"Probably not," she smiled. "And *New Silents* refers to the Silent generation before the Boomers, and probably won't stick for the same reason. But I read that America has been in a four-generation cycle that has remained unbroken for over four hundred years, except for the generations surrounding the Civil

War. Some have had good reason to take issue with their data. But they did predict back in 1991 what the Millennials would be like before they became adults, and in this case, they were right on."

He was fascinated and wanted to do more research on what she was talking about.

"Let's go with the Internet Generation," she continued. "According to their theory, iGen will be a smaller generation, overshadowed by the Millennials before them and the Boomer-like generation that will come after. They'll also be overprotected as children and will raise their own children in the opposite manner—like you Xers were. Overshadowed and overprotected, they'll be unsure and will find it hard to find a voice of their own. That's how the Silents, the generation before the GIs, got their name. On one hand, they'll be obedient and seek to improve on what the Millennials have built. Where Millennials were competent, iGens will become experts."

"Sounds insecure," he said.

"Right. But on the other hand, without a voice of their own, they'll be the most sensitive to the voice of others. If the theory holds up, their tendency will be to include more viewpoints and people. If Millennials are doers, then iGens will be improvers—making sure that society is equitable for all and that no one gets left behind. Martin Luther King Jr. and virtually every major figure in the civil rights movement came from the Silent Generation of 1925-1942. These iGens are supposed to be like them."

"Silent but just?"

"When you're in the ministry, it's far easier to see when someone or a group of people are being mistreated. So my guess for their spiritual question will be a little larger. I think it'll be, 'What is beautiful?' In part because their kind of generation usually produces great artists as well. A 2002 Stanford study showed that people judged the credibility of a website based on its visual appeal: if it was beautiful, then it could be trusted. But they'll also be skilled politicians, experts at due process, making sure everyone gets their fair shake. When society is beautiful, it will act in ways that include everyone. In that way, it'll be *just*. They'll try to correct the hubris of the Millennial generation and seek fairness and inclusivity for all. But according to generational theory, they'll do it in such a secular way that it'll create a spiritual hunger in the next generation."

He appreciated Bridge's rundown on the generations, especially of their spiritual questions of the day. But he wanted to know more specifically how this would relate to Jared.

Bridge seemed to anticipate his thoughts: "Now, back to your question. You asked me how to mentor someone spiritually today. Now that we have the generational background, can I show you what I use to disciple others?"

Stephen was about to say yes when Misun sat down on his armrest and patted his arm. He looked around and saw that they were the last ones there, and the Taylors had already started to clean up. They stood up, and Stephen gave Bridge a hug.

"Thanks for the talk," he said. "Can we keep this going?"

"Sure," she said. "Email me. We'll figure out a good time in the next couple of weeks. Why don't you take this?" she said, ripping off the first sheet on her notepad. "Can't do this with a tablet."

"You could've emailed it to me," he grinned. But he was still glad to have the notes.

Bridge gave Misun a hug and walked them to the bedroom. She watched Stephen pick up Brandon in his arms, while Misun scooped up Luke. With kids in arms and bags in tow, they walked to the car, buckled the kids in their seats and each gave Bridge a parting hug before pulling away from the Taylors'.

As he drove home, he told Misun about what he learned. Misun was surprised to see him so animated, and when she said so he whispered back as the kids slept in the back seat, "I asked her for help about Jared, but I have a feeling that it's going to help *me* out even more."

PART 1

Skeptic

LUNCH

Through email, Stephen and Bridge agreed to meet on Monday for lunch. No immediate deadlines were on the horizon at work, so he decided to take a longer lunch break to meet her at her office on campus.

The lunch commute from Rancho Bernado to La Jolla was surprisingly clear, and he made good time. After parking on campus, he found the campus mascot enshrined in a statue: a bronze version of the Greek messenger-god of the sea, Triton, holding a trident while blowing into a conch shell, all the while hovering over a waterfall. Her directions were good. He passed the statue and went up the many steps to the Price Center, where he found himself on a second floor balcony overlooking a cavernous modern food court. He took a right and saw Bridge's back through the clear glass wall that bounded her office. In the main student center, it was about as central a place as you can get on campus.

He knocked on the glass door, and Bridge got up from her desk and greeted him with a warm hug. The wall in front of him was covered by two whiteboards, side by side, with lots of scribbles on them from previous discussions and Bible studies. On the left side of the room was her desk, while piles of paper stood sentinel around her laptop. Around her desk, pictures of students from various ministry events covered the wall. In some pictures, the students wore long and big hair; in others, they were cropped and preppy. They clearly spanned the decades.

To the right was a larger lounge: a couple of couches, a small coffee table, a half a dozen folding chairs and another chair that was much more plush.

"Nice place," he said.

"A miracle," she replied. "We just got it. Our large groups meet right over there." She pointed over his shoulder to a red wall with the word *ballroom* in huge white letters.

"I didn't know how long the commute would be, so I didn't get a chance to pick up lunch. Want to go down to the food court?"

"It's okay. I already grabbed some," she said as she waved to the table. The coffee table had a tray ready with two sandwiches and a couple cans of soda. "We didn't say who was picking up lunch, and I thought it would save us some time. The left one's turkey, and the right is ham."

"Thanks, Bridge," he said as he sat on the couch. "I'll get you next time."

"You better," she said lightheartedly and then turned to erase the whiteboard. "Where did we leave off?"

"'How do you disciple someone?'"

"Gotcha," she said, as she drew an arrow.

$$\longrightarrow$$

"In the past decade or so, we've been using this," she said, as she pointed to the arrow. "It's a discipleship model, but so much more."

"Look what I brought," said Stephen as he waved his tablet computer for her to see.

She just shook her head.

"Jesus is the ultimate disciplemaker," she said. "No one did it better than him, and he launched a movement that would continue for two millennia, claiming a third of the world's population—about two billion of us, at least in name. So this diagram is the fruit of studying the way he did it and then trying to have it make sense in our context."

STUDENT

So let me start with this," Bridge said. "Discipleship comes from the word *disciple*. It literally means student, but it means so much more than sitting in a classroom and trying to get the grade. Back in Jesus' day, all Jewish boys would start to go to school when they were five, and many of them would have the Torah memorized by the time they were ten. I love the way one preacher puts it: 'Genesis. Exodus. Leviticus. Numbers. Deuteronomy. Memorized.'"

"Seriously?" said Stephen as he took another bite of his sandwich. "I don't think I could quote a whole chapter."

"It's an oral culture. Memorization came more naturally to them since they didn't have the Internet in their pockets to rely on. Still it happens today. I've had students who could quote all of *Monty Python and the Holy Grail* by heart."

"I fart in your general direction," he said with an attempted French accent. "Your mother was a hamster and your father smelt of elderberries."

"Exactly. At age ten, most kids would stop schooling and become an apprentice in their family trade. They'd learn to be fishermen, carpenters, shepherds. You get the picture. But those that excelled went to the next level of school, and the best students in this level had the rest of the Jewish Scriptures memorized by thirteen or fourteen. They'd also learn what other scholars said about the Scriptures. When they were fifteen, only the very best students were invited to be a disciple of a rabbi. The best of the best. A rabbi would come to one of them and say, 'Follow me.'"

"Fascinating. I didn't know they were that scholarly."

"The Galileans more so. I don't know why we think they were backwater hillbillies. Galilean scholars were more numerous, and often sharper and more devout, than their Judean counterparts. The Galileans pored over the Scriptures and were often the most zealous, so much so that they often revolted against the Roman Empire to reestablish Israel. Though Galilee was occupied territory, revolutionaries often came from there. It's why Nathaniel asks, 'Can anything good come from there?' They were often trouble."

Stephen wondered what it would be like to grow up in such a revolutionary environment. "Sounds like the Arab Spring movements or other uprisings going on these days," he said.

"Yeah," she said after a moment. "It would've been like that. So anyway, being a disciple was hard work. The goal of a disciple wasn't to get the grade, but to become like the rabbi and to do what he did. They were charged to 'cover yourself in the dust of their feet,' so that when they traveled with him on foot over dusty roads, they would literally be covered. Be with him always. Learn to be like him. Do what he does. If they trained well, they could become rabbis themselves at the age of thirty."

Jesus was thirty when he started his ministry, he thought, but he had a more pressing question: "The disciples, like James and John. They're actually supposed to do what he did? Even the miracles?"

"Right. Why do you think the disciples want to heal the sick and cast out demons? Why do you think Peter actually gets out of the boat to walk on water? His rabbi was doing it, and Peter knew, as his disciple, that he should be able to do the same kind of things. It was the very point of being a disciple. Now remember, the first four of the disciples were fishermen," she said.

"Yeah," he said absentmindedly at first. Then a smile started across his face in realization.

"They probably didn't make it past the first level of schooling," she said. "They were fishing with their fathers, learning the trade, remember? But Jesus still thought they could be like him. Jesus choose school dropouts and thought they could be like him. In that way, we often think about having faith in him, but here, he also had faith in us—that we could be like him and do what he did."

Jesus has faith in us? he thought. *Jesus thinks we can do what he did? That's either trust or madness.*

"If that's what it meant to be a disciple," she continued, "then we need to have that in mind when we disciple someone: we are not making disciples for ourselves. They're not my disciples, but his disciples. We are helping them become like Jesus in word and deed. So, here's how we've tried to identify the tasks of a disciple-maker in a simple way. Want to see it?"

He nodded as his fingers tapped quickly on his tablet. She knew she had him.

TRUST

Stephen turned around suddenly when he heard a rap on the window behind him. He saw two students wave at Bridge. She waved and smiled back.

"That must happen a lot," he said.

"I *love* this office," she said. "Now imagine this arrow as the life of a Christian. What we've done is divide this into five sections, each with its own title, and then we've identified what a disciplemaker should be doing at each stage. I know, it sounds simplistic, but it keeps things clear for what we do on campus."

"Simplify away," he said with some hesitation. He really felt like some focus would help him with Jared, but he also didn't want it to be too simplistic.

"The first stage is for a skeptic," she said as she wrote *skeptic* over the left-hand part of the arrow. "A skeptic is someone who not only distrusts Christians, but distrusts the motives behind what Christians do. Lots of people are like this today: one study showed that the new evangelists are atheists, highlighting an increasing trend of skepticism against the Christian faith. Many atheists and agnostics believe that radical Christianity is just as threatening to America as radical Islam. A lot of people are skeptical about the Christian faith, and it's hard for a skeptic to start training to do what Jesus did for the reasons he did them if he doesn't trust God or you. It's all about trust."

She wrote *trust* under the arrow, right under the word *skeptic.*

skeptic
~~*trust*~~ ⟶

"Wait a second. Your discipleship model starts with unbelievers?"

"Right," she said. "With both unbelievers and believers, we're just helping them become like Jesus and do what he did. We really see evangelism and discipleship as part of the same continuum. But we have different tasks at each stage."

"I like this. Some ministries focus on discipleship. Others focus on evangelism. This does both. But how do you build trust?"

"That's where I'm going. Millennials, remember, are a postmodern generation, so like the Xers, arguing for the faith won't work well. Remember that their spiritual question is, 'What is good?' They'll want to know if the faith delivers anything good to the world. So if I want to build trust with them, one part of it will be talking about a faith that brings blessings to outsiders and insiders alike."

"Gotcha, but that sounds a little like spin," he said. "What about just being in a relationship, just being friends. Won't that go farther?"

"You *are* an Xer, aren't you?" she winked. "Of course, all of this has to happen in relational trust. Be friends. Hang out. Don't be defensive. Don't be a jerk. Love. Serve. Pray. Yes, do it all. Most of all, listen. Hear where your friends are coming from. I think you Xers are pretty good at that, at least better than us Boomers, because you are built that way—more communal. It's also easy to break trust. Lots of Christians do it, because sometimes their lives don't live up to what they say. Jesus is the best example of integrity we have. He took his message of justice, healing and love all the way to the cross, and in the end he embodied loving ser-

vanthood and sacrifice for his followers. Ultimately, he said he
would come back to life, and he did. Thomas, the disciple that
was the most skeptical of Jesus' return, couldn't help but fall in
worship and adoration. So let your life match your words, and
admit when your life doesn't match up to your faith. You're right:
who you are—and who you are not—will speak more loudly than
any technique you might use."

"Gotta ask," he shrugged with a smile.

"Still," she said, "I think your generation wants to keep it relational and leave faith at the doormat because you think it'll break
too much trust. But it's not just about *relational* trust. It's also
about building *communal* trust—credibility for Christianity as a
whole. Humbly show how being a Christian is precisely why you're
able to bless your family, to reconcile your friends, to seek justice
in your communities and to seek good in the world. You don't
need to hide that stuff away with the Millennials."

"What is good?" Stephen replied, more as a statement than a
question.

"The first step in trust is to listen," she said. "It's a powerful way
to love. Have you asked Jared about his spiritual background yet?"

So obvious, he thought as he shook his head.

CUP

Tuesday came quickly, and Jared was in Stephen's office during the lunch hour. Stephen felt that the office would be better for intimate conversation, though Jared clearly had few misgivings about being open. Stephen reclined in his chair, while Jared was on the other side of the desk, sitting on the edge of his seat.

"What's your spiritual background?" Stephen asked Jared, thankful to Bridge for the conversation starter.

"I didn't grow up in the church, if that's what you mean."

"Sure, start there. Or start at the beginning."

"1990 was a big, *big* year," he said slowly with a huge grin. "A baby was born in Riverside . . ."

"Punk," Stephen said flatly.

". . . and the people all gathered around to see how incredibly handsome he was."

Stephen didn't have to roll his eyes.

Jared then started telling his story in earnest: "I grew up without religion. Both of my parents grew up in church but they didn't like Christians and didn't go to church by the time I was around. Every time Christians did something dumb on television, my folks would make fun of them mercilessly. So I picked up that attitude. I didn't want anything to do with religious people, especially if they were going to be so judgmental. How do you picket at the funeral of a gay man? Or burn the Qur'an? Or be so political? They didn't seem to have a clue about what's going on in the real world."

Stephen nodded, and Jared continued.

"I picked up a lot of my parents' values. In high school, the school board proposed to remove the busing program. So I helped with a campaign to fight against it. I wanted to keep our schools ethnically diverse. I even made speeches to the school board. We eventually lost, but I got an honorary membership from the Riverside Urban League."

He rolled up his sleeve to show his tattoo. "To remind myself to do what is right, I had an equal sign tattooed on my arm. Equality, right? Justice. It was huge for me. And I was shocked that Christians in my school didn't care. So when I came to college, I didn't care for Christians. I wanted to learn, but also have fun, date a little . . ."

"A little?" said Stephen.

Jared's smile brightened with even more wattage. "What? You couldn't tell? I looked forward to a new life. So after a semester, I rushed Sigma."

Stephen expected a huge smile after that, but Jared's eyes didn't have the same brightness. They almost seemed sad.

"We held mixers with a few sororities," Jared continued, "and I started dating this girl from Beta Phi. That time in my life felt like a blur, going from party to party. But it got old fast. My girlfriend dumped me for another fraternity brother. So I found someone new. Then someone else. And someone else. I couldn't be alone. I drank too. Who didn't? Classes weren't hard, so my grades didn't suffer much. But I didn't care about what I was doing. After a year and a half of that, everything started to feel, well, *blah*."

Stephen listened intently, surprised by Jared's self-awareness in telling the story. He took a quick look at his computer screen for the time. They had plenty of time.

"In the first week back at school, I get a knock on the door of my apartment. I open the door and this cute blonde is standing there. I have no idea what's going on. I just say, 'Hey,' and I'm checking her out a little bit."

Stephen unconsciously frowned and Jared picked it up right away. "Like you never checked anyone out!" he laughed. "She tells me that she's in the same apartment complex, and she's inviting people to something called 'Soma.' Sounds like a drug, right? I thought, *Party!* My roommates come to the door, egging me on, so I said we'd go. Thursday night. Her name's Audrey, and she says she'll come and get us before dinner. And I was like, 'Cool.' So she shows up with another guy, Tyson. Bummer, right? And we go out to dinner with *nine* other people. Two roommates bail, so only Alan comes. We hang out, it's good, they laughed at everything. Then we go to this Soma thing and I sit near Audrey. I found out that Tyson wasn't her boyfriend, just a co-leader of what they called a 'small group.' And I look around and there are maybe a couple hundred students there. Then I realize that I'm in a religious meeting. I was screwed."

Stephen grinned. "They really didn't tell you?"

"She might have said it. I can't remember. But I didn't really ask either."

"Was it a good experience for you then?" asked Stephen.

"No," said Jared quickly. "I looked for a way out. But we're sitting near the front, so I'm trapped. I sit through the band, and they're not half bad. Then the announcements got really goofy. Skits and stuff. I thought I was watching Nickelodeon or something."

Stephen unconsciously let out a snort. When he thought about his campus ministry experience, it had felt like it was caught between two worlds: the silly youth group and all of its exuberance on one hand, and the grown-up solemnity that covered topics such as social justice and racial reconciliation. He'd witnessed pie eating contests and goofy costumes during announcements, and then a call to radical living in a self-centered world later in the night. It was jarring. He thought that the steady stream of seniors leaving the fellowship was, in part, because the youth group stuff wasn't connecting anymore.

Jared continued: "But when the speaker came up, he asked us to keep an open mind. He seemed like a good guy, and I'm always open to new things. And I liked how he didn't hide behind religious language. He just talked about faith as if it were the most natural thing. I remember his talk to this day: It was on thirst. He pulled out a red plastic cup, and then he pulled out a Big Gulp, and then he pulled out a Double Big Gulp. The point was that no matter how big the cup we get, we'd still be thirsty for more. We'd never be satisfied unless we find God in our lives. Then he talked about how Jesus fills that need. Jesus can give us living water so we don't thirst anymore."

Stephen's eyes never left Jared's. He was hearing the earnest story of someone who was starting a new journey of faith. He rarely heard about people coming to faith anymore. He was reminded that people do change, and with each word in Jared's story, time lost its marchlike step. The work on his computer screen was the last thing on his mind.

"That red cup messed with me. How many times did I hold that red cup at fraternity parties? And he was right. It didn't satisfy. I wanted something more, like the lady he talked about that wanted 'living water.' I wanted what she had. I wanted what they all had. So at the end of the night, the speaker had people turn down the lights, the band started to play, and he asked us to make a decision to follow Jesus. In front of everyone. Crazy, right?"

Stephen felt his heart beat a little more strongly, swept up in the story of someone coming to faith. Jared could tell a good one.

"What he was saying seemed so good. But I wasn't going to stand up in a room full of strangers. He asked for a response a few times, the moment came and went, and I'm still in my seat."

Stephen tried not to look disappointed.

"It was good for them to ask. If they really believed it, then they should ask. I just wasn't ready. I didn't know anybody. And me, becoming a Christian at that point? No way. I didn't want to join the freak show."

TRADE

Stephen gaze didn't wander to the computer screen as he continued to listen to Jared's story.

"We hang out a little bit afterward at some restaurant," said Jared, "and that was it. No grand encounter with God. Nothing. And I went home, and nothing felt different. I went to a religious meeting, and I'm still the same guy. I thought that was the end of it."

"But something happened?" asked Stephen.

"Yeah," he smiled. "Audrey wouldn't leave me alone. I really didn't think she would keep coming around like that, but she did. I didn't mind. She was cool. When it came out that I felt tricked into that first meeting, she didn't just apologize. She asked for my *forgiveness.* Serious, right? I don't know many people who care about others like she does. Sometimes we'd just study. Other times we'd just talk all night, about anything and everything. Even religion. She was really easy to talk to."

"She sounds great," he said with a little suspicion.

"Yeah. After a little bit, I trusted her with anything. We'd hang out here and there, and then she invited me out to an event that her group was having. I asked her to explain what the meeting was about, and she was super clear. They were doing some project to raise awareness about sex trafficking and why Christians were involved in fighting it."

"I get excited. I say, 'Aren't you guys Christian?' And she's confused. She doesn't know what I mean. So I say, 'You're Christian, but you care about these people? I thought it was just about getting into heaven. I didn't know you cared about this kind of stuff.' And you know what she does? She gets all mysterious and says, 'Come and see.'"

Jared began unconsciously rubbing his tattoo as he continued with his story: "So I go. And it's *sweet.* There's no bait-and-switch. They really cared about the issues. Understood it. Gave money and time so that others would get to know more about it. They put on this incredible project that helped me understand what was going on and why Jesus cared about it. And I thought, if they're interested in doing something that helps the world now, I'd be more open."

They built communal trust, Stephen thought. He was glad to have a category for that, for what the ministry did with Jared while he was a skeptic. Now he felt that it would be foolish not to look at the time, and he saw that the lunch hour was over. He wanted the story to continue, but he knew that they should to get back to work on the new project, if they didn't want to be stuck at the office late for another night.

PART 2

Seeker

FRUIT

The next Monday, Stephen left work a little early to meet Bridge back on campus. He put some change into the parking meters in the shadow of the Marshall Lowers apartments and walked along the west side of the library.

Geisel Library was hard to miss. Named after Theodore Seuss Geisel, otherwise known as Dr. Seuss, it was the most recognizable building on campus. It was set on a hill, like a stage, in the center of campus, and its likeness became the logo for the entire university. To Stephen, it reminded him of a hand reaching out for fruit, like the tree of the knowledge of good and evil. It seemed more than a coincidence that the fruit in this case was the campus's largest library—a vast accumulation of humankind's knowledge.

He then took a Bridge-designed detour into a grove of eucalyptus trees. After he stood still and the ground ceased crunching underfoot, he swore he heard music and voices. As he looked closer at one of the trees, he saw that the voices were coming from holes in one particular "tree," which was encased with lead. He later learned that it was called the "Literary Tree," an art installation that broadcast poetry and verbal essays. Another "tree," the "Music Tree," played the music. These two stood like ghosts among nature's life, making the forest seem enchanted.

He walked out of the grove to the third tree of the collection that stood at the library's entrance. It was dubbed the "Silent Tree," presumably because it didn't make sounds like the others. He was supposed to meet Bridge here, but she was nowhere to be found.

As he looked around, the words above the entrance of the library caught his eye: "READ. WRITE. THINK. DREAM." Multi-colored windows surrounded the words, and within these panes the shadows of students standing on stacks of books were embossed in the glass. He later learned that the artist was referencing buildings in Europe where biblical saints adorned the walls. In this version, it's the students who are iconified. Of all the shadows, the girl standing to the left of "READ" seemed familiar, but he couldn't quite place it.

A few moments later, Bridge came up to him from his right.

"Sorry I'm late. You ready for the next stage?" she asked.

"Definitely," he said.

They took a leisurely stroll down the main walkway on campus as the lengthening shadows hinted at the coming sunset. It was beautiful, and he was thankful that Misun gave him some time to see Bridge again. On his left, he could see the slope down to the Price Center. Like a giant bowl, the bookstore, a theater, and a handful of restaurants and other meeting spaces surrounded a sunken courtyard full of tables and chairs. It was a great place to hold an outdoor gathering.

"Remember where we left off?" she asked.

"Skeptic. And the disciplemaker is to build trust. Not just relationally, but also as a whole. We're recovering the credibility of the Christian community."

"Perfect," she smiled with pleasure. "No folio while we're out walking, so think of the arrow in your head. Now add the word *seeker* along the arrow. A seeker is someone who trusts a Christian," she continued, "and begins to explore the faith. The overarching thing to get here is that you're not building trust with a skeptic anymore. Don't get me wrong: you still can do something really stupid to break trust. But if they trust you and what you stand for, then they may be ready to hear what you have to say."

He nodded as he brought the diagram into his mind's eye.

Bridge continued, "Most churches treat all outsiders in the same way. They often don't make a distinction between skeptics and seekers. So *grace-heavy* churches continue to build trust with them. They host events, parties and dinners, and they continue to build relationships. But they aren't helping their friends get to know Jesus more. On the other hand, *truth-heavy* churches just hammer away. They think if they don't wake you up to your sin first, then you won't listen to the good news they have to share. The problem with the grace-heavy churches is that even with trust, they don't move forward. The problem with the truth-heavy churches is that no trust is built in the first place, and so they are disregarded. Both fail to count the difference between skeptics and seekers."

"That would put me on the *grace-heavy* side." Stephen knew it. He loved getting to know people on their terms and prided himself on being connected with all kinds of people at work, whether they are gay, atheist or Muslim. He really loved interacting with people who were different than him. Sure, being with new people drained him a bit. But still, he really loved hearing a new perspective, and it was this learning instinct that kept him engaging people who weren't like him. He just didn't like to do it in large groups and preferred being with a smaller group of people so they could get past the small talk and get to the stuff that, in his opinion, really mattered.

"Of course you are," she said, with a grin. "So now that you have trust in this area, you need to challenge them to next steps.

So, on the diagram, to challenge them toward next steps is the task of the disciplemaker."

Stephen placed that along his mental diagram:

skeptic   seeker
trust   challenge   ⟶

"First, you challenge them with your *life,* trying to provoke curiosity."

That feels a bit manipulative. He hated things that felt too intentional, too programmed.

ACTION

Bridge!" a group of students shouted from a little distance. They hurried to close the gap, and Bridge gave them each hugs. They were heading to dinner and asked if Bridge wanted to join them. She said she couldn't and then introduced Stephen to the students. He noticed how much energy they had. Then the students turned and left toward the Price Center, while Bridge and Stephen took a right on Gilman Drive.

"You know everyone here," said Stephen. He already felt a little drained by the crowd of students.

"I wish," she said, with a smile. "There are always more to meet!"

"You are in the perfect job," he said. *I wish I could say the same about my own.*

They turned right up a hill, where buildings were found nestled in large groves of trees. The air felt cooler under the canopy of leaves and branches. As they walked, Bridge pointed out Mandeville auditorium and mentioned that they had their first large group meeting of the year there. Then she continued talking about the *seeker* stage.

"Even though they trust you," she continued, "it doesn't mean that they're *ready* to take the next step. They can trust you and yet not be curious about your faith. Mutual respect is there, but they aren't really keyed in to any spiritual journey of faith at this point. This is where many communities of faith miss it. They trust you, but you haven't done anything else to provoke curiosity.

Again, as you live an authentic life in Jesus, you might have something that they will become genuinely curious about. But I would suggest that you continue to find ways to show how God works in your life by telling your own story. A mentor of mine always said, 'Actions are not self-interpretive.' If you make sacrificial choices that serve others, instead of having them think you're just a good guy, you can talk about the ways God moved in your life up to that moment. You have to be intentional."

Again, that word, he thought. Stephen's shoulders tensed. He knew that he didn't talk about his faith with his neighbors, for instance. He kept it at the level of the weather, neighborhood schools and other easy talk. But he didn't let himself talk about God in a natural way either. He didn't want to turn people off unnecessarily and then have that mark on his soul for all eternity: *you* were the one who turned him away . . .

He valued authenticity, and intentionality felt like its very opposite.

Stephen then noticed a vibrant, multicolored statue that looked like a bird with a crest upon its head, high upon an arched pedestal, standing in the middle of a grassy clearing.

"What's that?" Stephen asked.

"Sun God," she replied. "It's part of an art collection called the Stuart Collection. So are the trees I told you about. The students now throw a festival in the Sun God's honor every year, and it's the biggest campus party of the year."

"Crazy. Sounds like a golden calf."

"Yeah, and we take some flak for coming out to the party. We take even more because we hand out water bottles to our often inebriated and dehydrated friends. It'll help with their eventual hangovers, and it allows us to build relationships on campus."

"Trust," Stephen recalled.

"Right, and some challenge. Students sometimes ask us why we're doing this. From there, we can start having meaningful conversations in the unlikeliest of places."

Stephen didn't say anything. He felt ambivalent about the idea. *Water for spiritual conversation? Really? Does this work? Even if it does, isn't it manipulative?*

Bridge had a hunch about what he was thinking. She had dealt with plenty of Xers in her ministry lifetime and knew he would react to her press toward intentionality. She didn't have that problem with Millennials, who just jumped in with two feet and tried it out. But Xers always needed a little coaxing.

"Let me tell you a story," she said.

"Sure," Stephen said slowly. He knew he was going to be set up.

TRIP

A couple of months ago, it was my twenty-fifth wedding anniversary," said Bridge, as they continued to talk.

"Yeah, I remember," said Stephen. "Congratulations again!"

"Thanks. But I don't think I told you what Lyle did." When Stephen shook his head, she continued. "He told me ahead of time to keep the weekend free and to get my bags ready. So we were packed for a weekend by Thursday night, and then Lyle had to go to work on Friday morning. But he came home around three and told me that we were off. I asked him where we were going, and he said, 'You'll see.'"

Bridge smiled large, as if she was experiencing the day all over again. "So we loaded up the car and headed out. And we drove north on the 805. So I think I know where we're heading. 'Ah!' I said, 'we're going to Temecula, right?' They have lots of vineyards there, and I was thinking that he'd head east on the 56. He just said, 'You'll see.' He was having a blast too. When we passed the 56, I realized that we couldn't be heading to Temecula. Then I shouted my next guess, 'Carlsbad, right?' And he just kept on saying, 'You'll see.' And when we passed the windmill in Carlsbad, I realized I was wrong. Right when I guessed, 'Palomar Mountain!' he turned off and exited at Oceanside. So I said, 'Yup—I knew it. Oceanside. I knew it.'

"But instead of pulling into a home on the beach, he pulled into the Amtrak parking lot. We unloaded our bags from the trunk and rolled them into the train station. I still have no idea

where we're going now, and he won't let me see the tickets. All I
know is that we're heading north. I keep guessing of course, and
now my guesses are wild: San Juan Capistrano? Disneyland?
Downtown LA? But we keep going. I've never ridden this train, so
once we pass LA, I have no idea where it goes. Fresno? I stop
guessing out loud."

Stephen wasn't sure where they were going either at the
present moment, but they were now on a paved walkway. The
trees gave way to more open areas, with large lecture halls to the
right and apartments to the left. Bridge continued: "The train
meanders through land for a while but then comes back along
the ocean. It's beautiful. The sun is setting slowly over the ocean,
and its rays are streaming into our cabin. And it's here that Lyle
pulls out a couple of goblets—how he kept them from shattering,
I have no idea—and a bottle of cabernet. After he pours the wine,
he says, 'Happy anniversary,' and we clink glasses. And I remember
having the feeling that there is nowhere else I'd rather be, with
no one else." And as she said this, she wiped the welling tears
from her eyes.

"We have a great conversation, but when we stop in Carpen-
teria, I start trying to figure out where we're headed again. By
now, I think I know where we're headed, but I've been wrong
before. We could just as well keep going to San Luis Obispo, I'm
thinking. He's messed with me so far. When we reach Santa
Barbara, he says we're getting off the train. I'm giddy. The sun
hasn't fully set, and Lyle hails a cab. I ask where we're staying, and
he says, 'You'll see.' We head up the main street, and then after a
while we veer a block off and stop at a corner where there is a
two-story Victorian. We get out, and I realize it's a bed and
breakfast, and I love, love, love B&Bs.

"I start to cry, and Lyle puts his arm around me. Then we put our stuff in our room and head out to a wonderful Italian dinner back on the main street. During dinner, he pulls out his phone and starts to read emails from our two children about what they most love about our marriage. I'm about to lose it again in the restaurant. He can pour it on thick, eh?"

Stephen started to squirm a little bit. He started to feel guilty: he wondered how long ago he did anything this extravagant for Misun.

"It doesn't stop there. The next morning, we wake up to a wonderful breakfast. Our host cooks these wonderful blueberry and apple pancakes, where the apples are sliced thin and are seared on the bottom by the buttered pan. Drizzled with real maple syrup, they were a treat. And then Lyle pulls out the last stop. He gives me a large envelope, and I open it and it's a certificate saying that he will be my shopping valet. It's so funny, because in fine print, it says that he will always have a smile, carry all my bags and give me his honest and present feedback for anything I try on. I know how much Lyle hates shopping, so this is the greatest gift of all! And we enjoy a great day on State Street, shopping here and there. At least I do!"

Stephen broke eye contact and looked down sheepishly. How many times has he opted out of shopping with Misun? At the mall, they go their separate ways. He figured he'd done his duty just by showing up, so then he'd head to a coffee shop to read while she shopped with the kids.

"Here's the important part: we could've just done something natural on our wedding anniversary. I mean, we could've just gone with the flow that day. Since we love each other, we would've had a decent time. We would've woken up late. I probably would've done the dishes and cooked lunch, because Lyle doesn't like to do that kind of thing naturally. We might have watched a movie or taken a walk to the neighborhood park. We would've had a great time. But because Lyle took the time to be intentional with me, I felt loved."

Stephen was right to feel like he was being set up, but he was paying attention.

"People, especially Xers like you, often think that intentionality is being fake or inauthentic. But it's precisely because Lyle was intentional that I felt even *more* loved. Aren't we always intentional with the people we truly love—thinking of gifts that are perfect for them, thinking of ways to love them? Our intentionality shows that we are thinking about them when they aren't right in front of us. In fact, if you're not intentional, I wonder if you truly love that person at all."

Ouch, Stephen thought. She twisted the knife blade into his apathetic heart. Yes, he definitely thought that being intentional, particularly with people who don't know Jesus, felt somehow wrong. It was somehow inauthentic. But Bridge was calling him out: if he wasn't intentional, then he probably didn't truly love them. At the very least, that felt fair.

Bridge pulled out her phone and found her Bible app. "Jesus did the same thing. In John 4, it says that Jesus 'had to' pass through Samaria to get from Judea to Galilee. But he didn't have to, and most holy men didn't. They went around, rather than sully themselves with the Samaritans. Racist, right? But what does Jesus do? He takes a path that most don't. Then he asks a Samaritan woman for a drink. Again most holy men did not talk to women. She gets it, and says, 'You are a Jew and I am a Samaritan woman. How can you ask me for a drink?' He throws out a line that's sure to raise curiosity: 'If you knew . . . who it is that asks you for a drink, you would have asked him and he would have given you living water.' Each step is intentional. And all of it so that she would end up being like the rabbi and do what he did. Samaritans become followers of Jesus because of what she did. We need to be intentional—with Christians and unbelievers alike—because that's exactly how we show our love."

He took a deep breath and nodded silently in surrender.

BIRD

As they walked, Stephen noticed a weird sight: mini-statues of Rodin's *Thinker* and various Buddhas were all over the lawn, and all staring into dilapidated television sets. Bridge mentioned how it was yet another art installation from the Stuart Collection, poking fun at how traditions were being overturned by the ubiquity of television sets.

"Can't let our entertainment become our brains and gods," she quipped. "So, if they're not curious, be intentional to share about your spiritual life in a natural way. If they are, be intentional about their next step. Pray about it, but make sure you ask them to *do* something. You can invite them to a Bible study where they can ask lots of questions or a weekend conference. But I also suggest service opportunities. When we go down to Mexico or to City Heights for an urban project, we make sure to invite our friends who don't yet know Jesus. It's something that all can agree on—the working for the common good."

"That's a great idea," Stephen agreed. "They'd be able to learn about our heart, without some cheesy presentation geared directly toward them."

"Sure. It's about invitations and challenges at this stage when they are in the thick of deciding to become a Christian—and from what I've seen, this probably lasts only about three to six months. Again, the process could be longer for people to become curious and be open to change. But when they're actively deciding to become a Christian or not, it's not a long time. After that, it's like they're almost inoculated. They've already tasted, and they know it's not for them."

"Only six months max?" Stephen repeated. He couldn't believe that it would be so short. He wondered where his friends were.

"Yes, so it's important that you're sensitive to the Holy Spirit and that you make yourself available to answer their questions and to challenge them to the next steps."

"Like inviting them to service projects," he said.

"Yes," she replied. "But when they're ready, you'll want to be even more intentional to offer the greatest gift of all."

"I get being intentional," said Stephen, knowing what she was getting at. "But isn't that just being pushy?"

"Look, this is God's work," said Bridge, while trying to hide some growing exasperation. "He's the one who's going to change their hearts about this. You're just along for the ride. So you don't need to add any pressure on yourself or anyone else. So yes, don't be pushy. Through the Holy Spirit, figure out what God is already doing in their lives and call it out."

"How do I do that?"

His earnest question helped Bridge find greater compassion for him. "You know Jim from church? He's an avid birdwatcher. When we were in the parking lot last week, he points to the sky and tells me to look up. I see a speck in the distance. He says that it's a red-shouldered hawk. I ask how he knows. He says that you can tell by the call, that it's one of the most vocal birds in California. Right when he said that, it made a piercing call that cut through the breeze. Then he said, 'Look at the window.' He meant the underside of the wings. It was white, lined with black. As he pointed these things out, it became even more beautiful to me.

"Now, here's what I'm getting at. What did it take for my friend to know the red-shouldered hawk? It took study and time. He memorized the pictures in books and learned the calls online. He woke up in the wee hours of the morning, wore camouflage clothing so he wouldn't stand out and spent hour after hour standing still looking through binoculars, waiting for a glimpse of a bird. It's after all this practice that he was able to recognize a red-shouldered hawk from the parking lot of our church."

Then Bridge laid it in. "Some are called to be birdwatchers. But Christians are called to be God-watchers. And if we prepare through prayer and Bible study, perhaps we'll be able to recognize when God moves right in front of us in our friends' everyday lives. If we see him, then it's our joy to point it out. That's what we do in the lives of seekers. We are pointing out the ways God is reaching out to them and helping them interpret these events in their lives. We are God-watching for them, so that one day they can do the same for themselves and others."

Stephen never thought of his life like this, pointing out what God was doing in another person's life. He definitely wouldn't do this to someone who wasn't a Christian. *If* this was true, then this made evangelism so much more exciting. It was an adventure, instead of a script.

"Again, it's what Jesus did. In John 5, it says," and she closed her eyes and said it from memory, "'Very truly I tell you, the Son can do nothing by himself; he can do only what he sees the Father doing, because whatever the Father does the Son also does.' We're just doing the same thing. And when the Father decides it's time to help someone with the next step of becoming a Christian, we need to be ready."

MESSAGE

The sun hid behind the hill that oversaw Marshall Lowers, and Stephen could see his car in the short distance.

"But at some point, I'll have to share the gospel, right?" asked Stephen.

"Sure, there will be a time when you have to give a reason for the hope that you have."

"Do I need a script then?"

"Cynical, eh? No, not a script. But an outline might help, no?"

He liked the trust-building part, and even the invitations. But the actual sharing of the gospel often felt more like a marketing pitch than real Christianity.

Bridge wouldn't let up: "Have you heard of the Big Story?"

"Actually, yeah," Stephen said. He remembered a presentation at church from a UCSD graduate student named Tom. He learned it from one of his closest college friends, Caleb, who ministered back in Seattle. "You know, when Tom taught it, I didn't think much about it. But after hearing the spiritual question of the day, I can see why this might make more sense. This could be helpful."

"And that's just one way. There are others. But I like the Big Story because it's trying to answer that question: What is good? We share the Big Story to share about what Jesus has done, is doing and will do at the end of time—to make everything right again."

They got to his car. He didn't remember steering Bridge here, but it was getting late and dark. He started to fiddle with his keys.

He turned to Bridge: "Need a lift?"

SMALL

Stephen looked around at the movie memorabilia that hung on the walls. A large poster of Marilyn Monroe holding down her skirt over a drafty grate hung over to the right. Near the middle was Al Pacino as a Sicilian in his white suit, straddling a half-black, half-white background. Up in the left-hand corner, E.T.'s glowing finger stretched out to touch Elliott's, in homage to the Sistine Chapel. And close by, there was an autographed picture of Nathan Fillion—a nod to a short-lived but much-loved sci-fi Western series. Stephen blinked his eyes in the wake of the sensory overload.

He didn't spend time in places like this after work. Usually, he raced home to relieve Misun of some childcare duties so that she could cook in peace. But he asked for another special dispensation this day, wanting to have more time with Jared, so he invited him to hang out after work. There weren't many places he could take him. Hooters, near the office, was out of the question.

They sat in a polished, wooden booth with brass rails adorning the top of it. A waitress with far too many buttons on her suspenders took their orders and then came back with a couple of drinks.

After some small talk, Stephen asked, "Tell me the rest of the story. What happened after the trafficking campaign?"

Jared looked up, recalling where he was in the story. "After that, I went through a long process. Audrey was a good friend at that point, and our conversations turned more and more to faith and belief. I'd pepper her with questions, and she wouldn't get fazed. She didn't know everything, but she didn't get defensive. Then she would say things that would catch me off guard."

"Like what?"

"Well, one time, she asked me point blank: What's the vision of your life? Weird question, right? I just said, 'To be happy.' And I'll never forget what she said next. She said, 'Your vision of life is way too small.' At first, I was taken aback. It was the first time she challenged what I said, but she did it with such earnestness and openness that I didn't know how to respond. I mean, what do you say to something like that? She took an ice-cold cup of water and threw it on my face. So I asked back, 'Well, what is the meaning of life for you?' And she says, 'I can show you.' She pulls out her Bible, but I get nervous, so I say, 'What? Are you trying to convert me?' And I think I got to her. She was stunned. So I keep at it and say, 'Christians are a bunch of hypocrites. Look at the way they treat others. Aren't they supposed to love and forgive? But all I see is hate.'"

"Were you being honest?"

"Sure. I thought that, but I know it was unfair. But she doesn't give up. She says: 'Don't judge Christ by what Christians do. All of us fall short of who he is. But most of us are trying to be like Jesus, and he's still worth checking out.' And then she adds, 'Besides, what do you have to lose? You don't want to be close-minded about the whole thing. What if Jesus might be the very thing you're looking for?'

"It was her turn and she got me. i mean, I was open, but I was close-minded about actually seeing what the Bible says. So I made a decision and said, 'Okay, I'll check it out.'"

"That night, we studied John 1. There was Jesus, being all cool and stuff. And I saw the same line that Audrey said, 'Come and see.' She challenged me to start a journey of curiosity. Come and see. Check him out for a while. See if Jesus was for me. I trusted her, so I gave it a shot."

CLIFF

.

The waitress came by to see if they needed another refill, but they were barely into their drinks. Stephen sipped slowly while Jared was doing most of the talking. Both of them just covered the tops of their glasses and shook their heads.

"Audrey and I would study the Bible pretty regularly. She kept pulling me back to John. She said that she just wanted to introduce me to Jesus, and then I was free to make my own decision. It was actually cool. I never knew Jesus could be so cool. How he loved. Who he protected. Who he cared about. Awesome."

Stephen was surprised given his dislike of Christians that he'd be so open to Jesus.

"We kept studying it," he said. "Audrey asked if she could bring a friend to join us, and I say sure. She brings Tyson—of course. And we just talk into the night. I just got honest, in a way I haven't done with many people before, except maybe people I've dated. They heard me out: my mom was sick at the time, and I told them how scared I was about her, how everything in life seemed so fragile, and I asked how we were supposed to hope in a life this meaningless. They listened. I mean, they really listened. Then they wanted to pray for me. It was a little freaky, but I said I'd be open-minded."

"Pray?" asked Stephen. That was a surprising turn for him. Jared, at this point, wasn't even a Christian.

"Yeah. So they put their hands on me, like on my shoulders and stuff. It was a little weird. But they prayed these peaceful, gentle prayers. I felt like I was being bathed in something good. They asked God to give me comfort and peace. And I really started to feel more peaceful. It was awesome."

Wow, thought Stephen. He didn't think he could pray for people who weren't Christian. That felt off-limits.

"If it was already weird, it got weirder."

"In what way?"

"I've got my eyes open, but they close theirs. But in the middle of their prayers, Tyson just looks up at me. Our eyes lock. Audrey still has her eyes closed. Tyson says that he saw an image and that he thinks it's for me. He said he saw a big red cup. He saw me drinking from it and then turning it upside down. Nothing was in it. There a hand comes down to ask for the cup, but I won't let it go. Crazy, right? That cup again! I never told anyone about how that talk connected with me. How would he know?"

Stephen's eyes focused more intently on Jared's, trying not to betray the anxiety that was brewing within. He was torn, but he still wanted to hear every single word.

"Then Tyson says something like, 'I think you're thirsty. But you won't let God fill your cup. Why don't you let him fill it for you?' I remember pulling back and shaking my head at first. This was too much. But then, I also knew that I really, really wanted that. So when he asked me what I thought, I just blurted out, 'I want that.' Audrey looks up at me and at Tyson, and he's just looking at me like he was surprised too. Then Tyson says, 'That was God speaking to you.' And deep in me, I knew he was right, but it was hard to admit. But I just nod anyway. He started praying for me some more and after they said, 'Amen,' he asked me how I felt. I said I felt at peace, like something or someone was there with me. I couldn't place it. All I knew was that I wanted to know more."

Stephen smiled. He loved to hear the stories of other Christians when they did something good and well, and here were some of Jared's classmates, just loving him. That's how the body of Christ is supposed to work.

"So what did you do?"

"Well, I just said it. I said, 'I want to know what you guys have. How can I be a Christian?'"

ISLAND

Jared's hands were moving wildly as he continued to tell his story. His eyes were alive and bouncing with energy. He leaned forward as he spoke, as if he couldn't get the next words out fast enough.

"So they looked at each other. Then Audrey tells me that God designed the world for good, but we messed everything up—our world, our relationships and our relationship with God—by living selfishly for our own ends. But Jesus died for it all, and all of the junk died with him on the cross, and when he came back to life three days later, a new life was possible—here and in the life to come. We're forgiven. And one day, all things will be made right, but for now, we are sent together to be agents of healing."

"You remember all that?"

He smiled. "Well, I've heard it a few times since. But it still made sense to me even then. I wanted it. But I still needed some time to think about it. So I said that I wasn't ready to make a decision yet. They were cool with that too."

"After all that, you weren't ready?" Stephen asked. He couldn't help himself.

"You can't rush this kind of stuff, right? So I got involved with everything they did. Whenever they invited me, I said yes. Small group, large group, you name it: I was there."

"Were you afraid of anything?"

"Sure. I still didn't want to become one of them. I had all of these objections. What about other religions? Did I have to become Republican? Did I have to stop believing in evolution? What about suffering? Why would God let people suffer? I had all these questions, and they never shut me down. They let me ask question after question, and it was cool with them. I thought I was tiring them out, but they kept telling me that this is the stuff they live for. They loved it. And they were real, dude. I could tell that they really cared about me and wanted me to get to know their God. But since that prayer, I couldn't get enough. It was the red cup all over again. I mean, it was like I was thirsty, and I wasn't going to stop until I got my fill. It was as if God made me a promise, and I was going to find out if he was good for it."

They were only halfway through their drinks when the waitress came by again. They shook their heads, and she went to the next table.

"At large group, they talked about going to Catalina Island for spring break. My fraternity brothers would be bummed—we went to San Diego every spring break—but I knew I had to go. So I invited my brothers to come too, and a few went with me, including my roommate, Alan. I had no idea that we'd study the Bible for eight hours a day.

"We took the ferry out. It was beautiful. You couldn't even get to the campsite by car. The boat went right to the dock, which was connected to the camp. Awesome. Palm trees. The beach. Beautiful, though a little rustic. But dude, studying Scripture was amazing and intense. We just got a stack of papers with the Bible printed on it. Mark study. No verse or chapter numbers. Just the Bible. They gave us markers and colored pencils, and we marked up the pages. And yeah, lots of candy to keep us awake. We just went through it line by line. It was perfect for me: any question I had was fair game."

Stephen wanted to know more about this way of studying the Bible. It sounded intriguing, but he let the story continue.

"I learned even more about Jesus. He healed people. He challenged the religious powers of the day. He loved the poor and the outcast. He crossed cultural lines. This guy was amazing. But we came to the passage where we were wondering who he is. Is he a good teacher? Is he a priest? But it was clear that he thought he was God. That messed me up. How could Jesus think he was actually God? That blew my mind.

"On the last night, everyone was in the main meeting room. It's like a lodge with school pennants hung all around the rafters. The teacher that night, Matt, really made me think about it. If Jesus is who he said he is, then what did that mean for me? I mean, I was asking all kinds of questions up to that point, but the main question was simple: either Jesus was who he said he was or he wasn't. Just a liar. Or a dude messed up in the head. But most people in this room really thought he was God. And I had felt God before. He was out there. I just didn't know if it was Jesus. But everything just made sense. I can't explain it.

"So Matt had us all bow our heads. He asked anyone who wanted to trust Jesus and let him take over to stand. I tell you, my blood was pounding in my ears. I knew that I was supposed to stand up. I felt the same way I felt when Audrey and Tyson prayed for me, but so much stronger. But I didn't. No one did. So Matt asked again for people to stand, and this time, I swear I saw something. It's hard to explain. I had my eyes closed. And I saw Jesus. I mean, I really saw him. And he had his arms around my mom. Like he was telling me that he loved her and would take care of her. And that got me. I started to cry like a baby.

"I stood up. I looked around, and most people had their heads bowed. But Audrey just looked at me from her seat, and I looked at her. I was freaked out and completely at peace at the same time. Tears started to stream down my face. But I knew that I was doing the right thing. And they cheered for me, dude. I hadn't felt that good. Ever.

"Alan stood up too. But then Matt told everyone that was standing to come to the front. He said that the staff and other students wanted to help us understand what was going on. We were already standing, so I guess there was no way out. So we all made our way to the front, having no idea what was going to come next."

Stephen's glass was now almost empty, while Jared's stayed full. He didn't sip while telling his story.

"Audrey was already out in front when I started coming up," Jared continued, "and she just kept smiling at me. I swear she had tears in her eyes, but it was a little too dark to tell. She and Tyson led me outside. And there we were, underneath the full moon and the starry sky. It never looked so glorious before, as if it were made by a great artist."

Stephen raised his eyebrows for a moment. He was caught off guard by Jared's sense of poetry. He didn't think this excitable pup would be able to slow down enough to observe, let alone get caught up in wonder.

"And I was expecting something freaky, like, I don't know. Some sort of initiation rite or something. I mean, when we pledges became brothers, it was a huge ceremony. And this felt something like it. It was mysterious, and I didn't know what was going to happen next. Maybe we were going to sacrifice a wild buffalo or something."

Stephen laughed. He had heard about the buffalo on Catalina Island.

"But instead, they just asked me a question. They wanted to know what was happening for me when I stood up. So I explained what I went through, and that I wanted to be a Christian. I told them how I had seen Jesus and my mom. I told them that I knew that Jesus loved me. It was weird: right after that, I started wondering out loud if it actually happened. Maybe my imagination got the best of me."

Stephen also wondered the same thing. Jared's story had a lot of things that he was uncomfortable about, especially the stuff he was seeing and hearing in prayer.

"Then Audrey put her hand on my shoulder. I remember it, because it felt like a charge went off when her hand landed. She said, 'That was definitely God.' And I felt like her words cemented what I was feeling. She didn't think I was crazy. I knew I felt something that was more than just biology or chemicals in my brain. It was something real. And having her say that was awesome. So she just gave me a huge hug. And so did Tyson. And they let me know that Jesus is throwing a huge party for me right now. And I just smiled. I couldn't believe it. I'd become a Christian.

"Then she said something rather freaky, but really cool. She asked me if I ever asked to receive the Holy Spirit. Of course I hadn't. She then said that when we become a Christian, God's Spirit lives in us. Our bodies become his home. So she just wanted to pray for that. I said sure. Sign me up. God living in me? Way cool.

"So they started to pray, and they asked God to fill me. And I felt something like a weight fall on my shoulders. Everything became gloriously heavy. Not burdensome. Just real. And joyful. And full of peace. And it's so weird, but I just felt like I had to lie down. So in the dirt, under the light, I did. And rested. For the first time in my life, I just rested—soul, body, mind. All of it was still, at peace. And they told me that God was with me, and I knew it. I mean, it wasn't just in my head. I knew it for me. Right then and there."

Then he paused, looked Stephen in the eye and said: "He was with me."

PART 3

Follower

BEACH

Though the blue skies ushered in temps that hovered in the seventies, Stephen could've taken a day like this for granted. Most San Diegans would. When the mercury climbs above eighty degrees, it's easy to start a conversation with "Scorcher today, right?" When it drops below sixty, "Freezing, eh?" Blood runs thin in this town.

Still, the Santa Ana winds brought in warmer-than-usual temps for this time of year, and Stephen determined to enjoy this particular Saturday. He leaned forward in his beach chair and crushed the sand under his toes. He closed his eyes as the coastal breeze brushed his face and the rhythmic sounds of the waves lapped into his ears. He wondered, just for a second, if heaven would be this nice.

"Isn't this beautiful?" he said to no one in particular.

"Yup," said Misun. She sat next to him in another chair, not even bothering to look up from her e-reader.

"Daddy!" Luke shouted in distress. Stephen looked up and saw Luke running along the surf, with Brandon stumbling after him. Then he saw Jared marching after both of them, with his arms straight out and his hands curved into claws. "I'm coming for you!" he shouted. "The baptism monster is coming for you!" And the kids would shriek down the surf, laughing and screaming repeatedly, "I don't want to be baptized! Not again!"

Stephen grinned at the irreverence but caught himself before yelling, "You're making heretics of my kids!" There were too many other families about. Jared's faith was so open, so free. He could even joke about it. But for Stephen, that felt a little outside the bounds, like roaming around Moscow shouting things in English. He didn't want heads to turn.

It was great to be out at the Torrey Pines State Reserve with his family, and he was glad that Jared could tag along. The sandstone cliffs towered behind them, the surf was in front of them, and here, in contrast to other beaches, sun-soakers could spread out and enjoy a little space. It was gorgeous, and he just wanted to have a chance to interact with Jared in less formal ways. He should've known that Jared would be great with the kids.

Jared caught up to Luke, wrapped him up and tackled him slowly to the turf. Then he picked him up, dragged him out from the beach and dunked him underwater. When Luke came back up, he frantically scrambled closer to shore and then stood up in the surf, knees just above the waterline, coughing. He had taken in some ocean water, and he started to cry.

Jared picked him up and carried him back to Stephen.

"Sorry, dude," said Jared. No smiles now. "I didn't mean to . . ."

"Don't worry about it," said Stephen, as he examined Luke. "He looks fine." Misun looked up just enough to give Jared a cross look and then went back to her novel. Jared didn't fail to notice and turned up the charm.

"At least he's *holy* now," he said to Misun, smiling wide.

She couldn't help but smile. "Washed clean, right?" she joked, and then went back to reading.

Stephen hugged Luke and looked him in the eye: "You okay?"

"Uncle Jared's *mean*," he frowned.

"What did he do?" he asked, though he knew. Stephen was just getting him to talk.

"He baptized me."

Stephen stifled a laugh and mussed his hair. "Go and play," he said. He patted Luke on the butt, and then Luke dove into the sand toys.

A wet Jared sat down next to Stephen. "Seriously, I feel bad about . . ."

"It's okay, man. You should see some of the things I've done to them."

Stephen and Jared both stared out over the ocean. The waves sparkled like yellow flash bulbs popping over the tiny crests. Behind them, colorful paragliders floated their way down the coast, using the ocean winds that bounced upward off the cliffs. Out in the distance, they could see a ferry making its way out to Catalina Island.

"Remember going out there?" asked Stephen. He recalled the conversation they had at the restaurant a couple of weeks ago.

"Yeah, that wasn't too long ago."

"Do you still feel that God is with you?"

"Not all the time," he said, unconsciously rubbing his tattoo. "Am I supposed to feel that way *all* the time?"

Brandon waddled over to the family mat and tried to take a pail from Luke, but Luke gripped hard and gave him a shove with his elbows. Brandon started to howl. Misun looked up, instinctively grabbed a shovel and gave it to Brandon, who calmed down and started digging into the sand.

"No," said Stephen. "But God *is* speaking to us all the time, trying to get our attention."

"How does that work?"

PASTOR

Stephen was glad that he had met up with Bridge the Sunday before. On that day, he drove on the 52 West right into La Jolla Village Parkway. As he entered La Jolla, he had an elevated view of the ocean framed by houses dotted along rolling hills. He couldn't afford to live there, that's for sure. So when he pulled into his destination, he was surprised that Bridge's campus ministry leaders could meet there: a large church with palm trees dotted all the way up and down its sides, just a few blocks from the ocean. This was prime real estate.

After parking in the underground lot, he stepped into a quiet elevator. But when the doors opened on the second floor, the roar of a crowd of 120 college students caught him off guard. Bridge would later tell him that they couldn't secure a room large enough to meet on campus every Sunday night. So when a nearby church generously offered their building for free, Bridge was quick to sign up.

He stepped into the large meeting room and wondered at what point in his life college students started looking like they were in high school.

I'm getting old, he thought.

He spotted Bridge talking animatedly with a few other students. He waved and she nodded back, but the intensity of her gaze let him know that she was in a weighty conversation, so he let her be. Without anyone else to talk to, he took a seat in the back row.

Though there clearly was a youthful energy in the room, the murmurs felt heavier. The looks, more serious. If he had to put a word to it, the atmosphere felt *tense*. Still, he was glad for the invitation to come check this out. Bridge wanted him to see firsthand how she developed her students.

"Five minutes," Bridge said to the students, then went right back to her conversation.

Stephen pulled out his cell phone and realized that the meeting, by some act of God, was going to start on time. He didn't remember college students being so punctual either. He started to check his email when he felt the weight of someone's hand on his shoulder. He looked up and his eyes brightened in surprise.

"Pastor Rob! What are you doing here?" asked Stephen.

"I should ask the same of you!" replied Rob. Both Stephen and Bridge knew him as their senior pastor. He was relaxed, and the smile lines around his eyes were deep and plentiful. But it was his full gray head of wisdom that stood in great contrast, not only to his own rich tan, but also to the youth bubbling all around him.

"I love young people," Rob said, looking around, "especially the ones in college today. I love their can-do attitude."

"So you're a fan?" said Stephen.

"They listen way better than you guys did, that's for sure. Sometimes they don't know their fingers from their toes, but they really think they can change the world."

Stephen grinned and Rob smiled back. He said in a lowered tone: "Plus, I'm here to make sure Bridge doesn't go off the deep end. It's a crazy time on campus, and I want to support her, of course. But I also want to see how she does this prayer thing she always talks about." Rob raised his eyebrows and gave a slight nod, gauging whether or not Stephen was in the know. When Stephen stared back blankly, Rob moved on.

"By the way," Rob said, "Bridge says that we're going to grab some dessert afterward to talk it over."

"Looks like she's got you under her spell as well."

"She's powerful that way," said Rob. "She won't even let me speak during these meetings, unless she calls on me. She wants the students to figure it out. I hope it turns out well."

Stephen was about to ask what was happening on campus when Bridge spoke up over the crowd.

"Let's pray," she said.

LISTEN

After the opening prayer, Bridge said, "You all know what happened last week on campus. So we need to figure out how to respond as a fellowship. I asked all of you to fast your dinner before coming so that we can be ready to hear what God might have to say. So tonight, we're scrapping our normal plans. Instead of going straight into teams, we're going to spend some time in prayer to find out what we should do next. Cool?"

The students murmured in agreement. She introduced a prayer topic, then had students pray. For the first topic, they praised God; students offered one word of praise out loud, one at a time, until the praises rose to heaven like floating embers. Then she led them in silent confession. The prayer time felt more structured and formal than what he'd seen at church. Next they all prayed out loud at once, which created a holy rumble that flowed throughout the room. Then they prayed one at a time.

From these prayers, Stephen got a sense of what had happened on campus. A fraternity, with mostly white members, decided that it would be funny to host a party called the "Compton Cookout." The fliers he'd see later were clearly offensive: the boys were to come dressed in baggy athletic wear, while the girls were to wear "gold teeth, start fights and drama . . . have short, nappy hair . . . and speak very loudly." To a shrinking African American student community at UCSD, due to the repeal of affirmative action throughout the university system statewide, it felt downright hostile.

Overnight, this sleepy campus became the center of outrage and action. Hundreds of students came out to the Price Center, many from other schools, demanding reforms. They received national media attention. In the aftermath, racial tensions that had rumbled beneath the surface now erupted. A racial epithet was broadcast on student television. A noose hung from a bookcase in the library. These incidents poured a truckload of salt in an already festering wound.

The administration hosted a "teach-in," hoping to address the concerns of the protests. But they didn't include any student leadership from the black community in the decision making and had merely invited the BSU's president to say a few words at the start of the rally. It smacked of paternalism. So when the BSU president came up to speak, she used the opportunity to stage a walkout, and the campus was further divided. Bridge's campus parachurch ministry, although made up mostly of white and Asian students, felt compelled to respond. But in this powderkeg environment, the fear of making a mistake loomed large.

They had prayed fervently. Stephen couldn't help think that faith was being passed on well to a new generation of rising leaders. In this room, students of vibrant faith wanted to see God's kingdom come. But what Bridge did next unnerved him.

As the frequency of prayers died down, Bridge said, "Let's take some time to listen to God. We usually make speeches to God, but don't often stop to listen. Prayer isn't monologue. It's dialogue. God is speaking. So take some time to listen. This isn't an emptying of our minds. For Christians, we wait in anticipation to hear God speak. And something may come to mind. It might be a Bible verse, an image, a song, a word, a feeling, an impression. It can come in many ways. But as it comes, don't shut it out immediately.

Reflect on it. If you don't know what it means, ask God about it. And wait again. You might not hear anything. That's fine. That doesn't say anything about you or the level of your faith. He is a person and can speak if he wants. Or he may stay silent, if he thinks that's best for now. God doesn't have to answer. We're just putting up the sail, so if Spirit's winds decide to blow we can catch it. Let's take some time."

Stephen looked around to see how students were responding. He saw bowed heads. Some eyes were open; others were closed. No music played. All were silent. All were still.

WATER

After what seemed only a short moment, Bridge then asked, "What did you hear? Take a risk and give it a shot. We have enough people with gifts of discernment in the room to help you figure out if it's from God or not." Stephen was surprised by how *un*emotional everything was. It was just matter-of-fact.

After a few moments, a student stood up and said, "I see a banana."

That's silly, though Stephen. He looked at Rob to see what he was thinking, and when their eyes met, Rob just shook his head. He waited for Bridge's correcting word, but he was surprised by what she said next.

"Okay, and what do you think that means?"

She's going with it? thought Stephen.

"I don't know. I just thought I'd share it."

"If that's from God, then there'd be more," Bridge said. Stephen exhaled a little too loudly, while his shoulders relaxed. "Here's a tip," she continued, "when you read the prophets in the Bible, like Zechariah, you'll see that when they see an image, they keep asking God for its meaning. Amos once saw a basket of ripe fruit. You would think, from first glance, that it would be a good thing. A reminder of harvest or Thanksgiving, right? But God basically says that the time is ripe for judgment. Not exactly what you'd think at first, right? So keep asking. Try to see if you get any more interpretation from it. But I'm glad you took a shot at it."

Though Stephen was glad for the correction, he was still confused. *How did she know?* Also, the student seemed to receive her admonishment with ease. A few more moments went by. Then another student raised his hand and said, "I just see a giant cloud. I can't see where we're going. And maybe God might be saying that we should stay away from this issue."

Murmuring erupted, and Stephen could sense a rising tension in the room.

"What were you feeling when you saw it?" Bridge asked.

"Fear. I was afraid."

"Thanks, Peter. It's great that you put that out there. That image may be from God, but I think your image is still incomplete. Remember, 'perfect love casts out fear.' So if it's from God, fear shouldn't be a part of the equation. Since you were afraid, I'd want to double-check your interpretation. Even if the image is from God, the fear leads me to think that there might be another way to look at that image. Staff, what do you think?"

She looked around to her other partners in ministry, and one spoke up: "When I think of the image of cloud in Scripture, I think of God's glory coming down, leading his lost nomadic people into the land of promise. That's a little different than what Peter said."

"Okay," Bridge said. "There's enough here to question that interpretation. But Peter, keep trying. It's great that you put it out there. Anything else?"

Stephen felt his trust of the process rising. At first, he thought the students had way too much freedom to share what they saw. How would they know if it was from God or not? They could say anything. But Bridge not only directed the time, she also gave biblical reasons for correction. Now Stephen wanted to learn how she was discerning what was from God and what wasn't.

An Asian woman stood up, and she seemed a little older than the rest of the group. "Okay," she said. "This is weird. I see a waterfall. And the water is rushing down and then over the land. The land is parched and cracked. And as the water covers the land and falls into the cracks, flowers spring up, like at Anza-Borrego. It's a desert bloom."

Bridge thanked Serena and asked if anyone else saw something similar. Another student said that he saw the same thing. A tall blonde man with curly locks stood up and said, "I just saw a glass of water, and it was being given to a really ragged and thirsty dude. And he drank from it, and the water didn't run out. He just drank until he wasn't thirsty anymore."

Two more hands went up. They saw something similar.

"I think we have some confirmation," said Bridge. "Water. Refreshment. What do you think it means?" She directed this question back to the first student.

"I think," Serena said with some hesitation, "that God wants to bring refreshing to the campus. That he wants to bless it and make flowers come up where we thought nothing would bloom."

A Latino student with a plaid shirt stood up: "I'm not sure about this, but all I heard was, 'Psalm 126.' So I looked it up, and this is what it says: 'When the Lord restored the fortunes of Zion, we were liked those who dreamed. Our mouths were filled with laughter, our tongues with songs of joy. Then it was said among the nations, "The Lord has done great things for them." The Lord has done great things for us, and we are filled with joy. Restore our fortunes, Lord, like streams in the Negev. Those who sow with tears will reap with songs of joy. Those who go out weeping, carrying seed to sow, will return with songs of joy, carrying sheaves with them.'"

"I've been reading the Psalms!" said Serena.

Bridge was about to remark, when Pastor Rob's hand went in the air, waving intensely. Stephen thought he detected a glint of disapproval in her eyes. She looked for other hands before eventually calling on him.

"I know you asked me not to speak, but I think this'll help," he started. The students laughed, both at Bridge's boldness and this pastor's inability to keep quiet. "That psalm is exactly what Serena talked about. The Negev is a desert, and there, streams would come without warning, like a flash flood. But after the streams came, the desert would bloom with flowers in its wake. The image speaks of a sudden blessing that comes unexpectedly. So, you didn't know about the Negev?" He directed his last question at the student in the plaid shirt.

He shook his head while murmurs of agreement filled the room. Stephen felt the edge of his hair stand on end, as if some electric current surged through the air. He was paying full attention, and it was as if the room was holding its breath in anticipation.

Bridge nodded slowly. Stephen could see that she thought his comment was truly helpful, and he was genuinely amazed how these images and visions were lining up.

"Yes, I think that's from God," said Bridge. "He wants to bring blessing to the campus in unexpected places. And this would be one of those times."

If there was any hesitancy in the room about addressing the campus crisis head on, it was gone. It was as if someone poured an oil of gladness into the room, and there was a deep sense of unity and encouragement that wasn't there before. More images, Bible verses, and other words were shared. After the prayer,

Bridge said that the student leadership team would need to meet during the team meetings, and she dismissed the other teams to plan how to be a blessing to the campus community during this crisis.

As the students filed out, Stephen leaned back in his chair and glanced over at Rob. He was flipping intensely through the pages of his Bible.

DESSERT

Bridge, Stephen and Rob walked a few blocks from the church and sat near the back of a crowded French-inspired café. An assortment of pastries and a trio of coffee mugs held court on the table between them. Though it was a little stuffy inside, the glass wall next to them afforded a beautiful view of the setting sun over the ocean. The windows were slightly ajar, allowing the quickly cooling ocean breeze to waft in.

"I've never been in something like that before," said Stephen.

"You mean the listening prayer?" said Bridge.

"Yeah, and to see them responding that way. It was wild."

"You really did a great job leading it," said Rob to Bridge, "though I also had some questions about it."

"You always do," she laughed. "But I'll take the compliment. It wasn't always like that. It took time to build a culture that listened to God. But once it did, it was amazing. In motivating students, one word from God is worth a thousand sermons. Like tonight, if we went straight to planning, I'm sure we would've had a revolt. Race is a scary topic for these guys."

Stephen could only nod his head in agreement.

"So we started with prayer meetings every weekday on campus. But we added listening prayer as well. Then, we'd have to act on what we've heard to test it. Lots of ministry started from that place. One student heard that she was supposed to start a Bible study in a particular dorm, and she did with some other students. Other students changed majors according to what they heard.

Others were told to reach out to particular campus groups. And the prayer meeting thrived. It was energizing."

"But aren't you afraid of people just following their own whims?" Stephen asked. "I mean, how do you know that all of this stuff is from God?"

Bridge suddenly looked up, and Stephen felt a pang of guilt. The question came out far more accusatory than he had intended. He responded quickly. "Sorry, I didn't mean it that way. But I am truly curious: How do you discern whether it's from God or not?"

Rob crossed his arms and joined the chorus: "That's exactly what I'd like to know too."

"Sure," she said a little wearily. It had been a long week on campus, and defending her theological or ministry positions against two men didn't feel energizing at all.

WORD

Bridge exhaled and looked out at the ocean through the glass wall for a moment to find inspiration. Then she continued: "Most discernment is rather straightforward. I go by four things. It doesn't help you with every call, but it can deal with most."

"Mind if I take notes?" Stephen had already pulled back the cover on his tablet.

"Sure," she said, feeling slightly better that he wanted to learn. "The first is obvious: Is it biblical?"

Of course, Stephen thought. Rob nodded his head in approval.

"In Acts 17, the Bereans were considered of more noble character because they tested Paul's message against the Scriptures every day. He won't contradict his Word. He doesn't change. In the most obvious example, if a voice tells you to murder someone, you can write it off as not from God."

"Ah, so you do believe in the Bible?" Rob joked.

"Just because you don't preach from it doesn't mean the rest of us leave it at the office!" she bit back. They both laughed hard, and she was grateful for the levity. But Stephen's eyes were wide with horror.

Rob laughed: "We joke like this all the time. I'm not sure where it started, but given Bridge's personality, you might have a good guess."

Bridge gave him a playfully cross look.

"You *both* have more personality than me," Stephen replied with a smile. But then he got back to the topic. "But that's an obvious example. What about something a little more neutral, like which job I should take?" He half hoped they might have a direct word from God for him right then and there.

"Sure, it doesn't answer every question," said Bridge. "That's where the community of faith comes in. We need to figure these things out together, with the Spirit's leading. Lots of times, we won't be absolutely certain. That's fine, though, because faith isn't about certainty. It's about trust."

COMMUNITY

Stephen tapped on his tablet quickly, as Rob listened on while biting into his chocolate croissant.

"So that leads to the second question," said Bridge. "If the first is, 'Is it biblical?' then the second is, 'What does the community say about it?'"

"Our friends?" Stephen asked.

"Well, yes and no," she said. "Not just any friend, but our brothers and sisters in faith. And sometimes, our friends are a better measure of what God might be saying to us. It's nonsense to think that we'll hear God better by ourselves, up in some mountainous cave. Yes, there are times to be alone, but when it comes to discernment, our community is crucial. In 1 Corinthians 14, it says 'prophets should speak, and the others should weigh carefully what is said.'"

Stephen nodded in appreciation. Too many people end up doing some unwise and silly things because they heard from God, even though everyone else is telling them not to do it.

"Think about this," she continued. "Students often talk about relationships, about finding 'the one.'"

Stephen's ears pricked up. He felt like this could be helpful for Jared.

"One of the greatest areas of deception for young single people is in the area of relationships," she said. "There's too much at stake, and our emotions cloud our judgment. And if the relationship becomes sexual, that creates another bond that is difficult to break, even though it would be better if they were apart. The Scriptures say that when you have sex with someone, it's as if you're married. The bond you've created is that strong. So it's hard for people to leave folks they know they shouldn't be with if sex is involved. Sex is like relational super glue: it sticks you to anyone else, even to those you don't want it to."

"I need to talk to a few couples in our church," Rob remarked.

Stephen could buy most of that, but still, that seemed to be a huge thing to say.

"What about people who have a string of one-night stands? It doesn't seem like they have super glue of any kind."

Rob smiled. He liked the way Stephen asked questions, whether here or on the elder board. He saw that others at church respected him for it.

"It still *sticks,*" she said. "Sex still bonds people. But those who go from person to person make the same bonds, then break them, then make them, then break them. Over and over. It damages them. When they finally want to, they find that it's much harder for them to actually stick. Those who stick and break constantly carry those scar-filled tears with them."

Stephen nodded. This kind of reasoning is more helpful than *God says so,* no matter how true it may be.

"So relationships are often places of deception," she continued. "We want to be with someone so badly that it becomes harder to hear God's voice objectively. So we need our community of friends who will talk straight with us. Even if they don't know the other person, they can tell how *you're* doing and how this person is affecting you. Is he pulling you away from your faith community? Is he becoming a part of it? Does she bring out the best in you? Or does she bring out the worst? Your friends, the ones who know you, can see if he or she is good for you or not. They are super-helpful in the discernment process, in a way that doing it by yourself will often leave you coming up short."

"Where two or three are gathered in my name . . ." Stephen started to say.

". . . there I am with them," she finished. "That passage is in the context of discipline, but still, there is something where God's presence seems to feel more, well, *present* when we are with the faith community."

"That would include the community that have gone before us, right? Like the 'great cloud of witnesses'?" said Rob.

"Yes," she said as she looked in his direction, "if something radically departs from Christian traditions, then we should also be wary of it. The community, past and present."

"Bridge," Rob said, "you might be converting me."

"Good," she joked, "because you definitely need to be right with God."

FEAR

Okay, we've got two: the Bible and community," said Stephen, looking down at his notes.

"The third is key," said Bridge, "and could be the most important: Does it cause fear?"

"I know you said that fear isn't good," Stephen asked. "But doesn't the Bible also say that we should fear God?"

"Right, but that's a different kind of fear. One of awe and reverence. But whenever God shows up, what does he say?"

Stephen racked his brain a little bit. But Rob jumped in.

"Don't be afraid," Rob said. "Fear not."

"And what often goes with that?"

"For I am with you," Stephen jumped in.

"Right," she said. "And that's it. If it's from God, it has that kind of spirit. It might freak you out at first, but it should have a calming effect. Don't be afraid. For I am with you. Remember what it says in 1 John? Perfect love casts out fear. And John says earlier in the same chapter that *God is love.* So," and here she used her best nerdy voice, "by transitive property, God casts out fear. When he shows up, fear is gone."

"So what does that mean in the discernment process?" said Stephen.

"If someone shares what he or she saw and it causes fear in the fellowship, it's probably not from God. Or, at least, it's not complete. If God brings up something that causes fear, then he will also find a way to quench that fear in his love. So if people start responding out of fear, then you have a message that is causing disruption and division. You can at least say that the message is not complete, but most of the time, you can just say it's not from God. Paul says that all prophecy is given for strengthening, encouragement and comfort. So that should guide us instead of fear. In many ways, we're trying to figure out what to do if fear was absent."

I could do this, Stephen thought. There were times when fear crept into the picture, and he knew that it wasn't from God, but he was too afraid to say anything. He didn't want to "quench the Spirit." But now he was being given some helpful tools to help with discernment, particularly within a community.

CHARACTER

Stephen looked for the *palmier* on the pastry plate, but it was empty. Instead, the curved pastry had found its way to Rob's hand, with a bite already taken out of it. Stephen tried to content himself with his cup of coffee and then shifted in his chair a bit to something more comfortable to type more notes into his tablet.

"So we got three," Bridge continued. "The last one is a little like the third one: What is the fruit?"

"What kind of fruit?" Stephen asked.

"You know what it says in Galatians 5 about the fruit of the Spirit?"

"Sure," Rob started, "Love, joy, peace, patience, kindness, goodness, faithfulness, gentleness and self-control."

"Our pastor knows his stuff!" said Bridge sarcastically. "And Jesus said that you know whether a tree is good or bad by its fruit. Does the person deliver the message with this kind of fruit? Or does that person become mean, sour, anxious, demanding, rude, forceful, suspicious or out of control?"

"So when I'm watching TV," Stephen said, "and see these guys yell God's message to a wider audience in a way that seems, well, like the last things you said, then you're saying it's probably not from God?"

"If it is as you say it is, then you can at least question their message. Or they're giving the message in the wrong heart, which will then discredit the message anyway. It should be given in a way that shows the fruit of the Spirit, or as Jesus says, they're a bad tree."

RECOGNIZE

She pulled out her folio yet again and placed it on the coffee table. Stephen should've known that the action wouldn't have surprised Rob.

She said to Rob, "I know you've seen this before. I'm walking Stephen through it."

She pulled the pen out of its tab, redrew the diagram that Stephen had seen up until now, and added the word *follower*.

"What should all followers of Jesus be able to do?" she asked. "It's actually not an easy question to answer. We usually have lots of answers. We want all Christians to be able to read the Bible. Pray daily. Go to church weekly, right Pastor Rob? Be a part of a small group. But if you were trying to make it simpler, what would you, as someone who is mentoring a new Christian, want them to do?"

Stephen shrugged, though he desperately wanted to know what she would say. He had asked the same questions. He thought she had asked another rhetorical question, but when Pastor Rob and Bridge stared at him in silence, he blurted out: "Be like Jesus?"

He was surprised when she said, "Right!" But he should've known that the affirmation would be short-lived.

"But when we think about it," Bridge continued, "that's pretty vague. Everyone's picture of Jesus is often what they idealize or prefer. We rarely have the same picture of him. And then, even if we have a picture of him, we don't really know what to do to get there."

Stephen waited, knowing that the payoff would come.

"The point of our spiritual disciplines, the point of praying, the point of reading the Scripture, the point of being a part of a faith community—all of it leads to learning how to recognize God's voice in the everyday and to obey what we hear. We need to learn to hear his voice. Then we learn how to have the strength to actually obey what we hear. But I think we often focus on the second part without doing the first part."

Stephen blinked. He hadn't thought this is where she'd end up. But still, it didn't strike him as completely off.

"Let me read you a quote," she said. She reached down into her bag yet again and pulled out her smartphone. After a few button presses, she started to read:

"Dallas Willard says that 'People are meant to live in an ongoing conversation with God, speaking and being spoken to. . . . Given who we are, we live—really live—only through God's regular speaking in our souls and thus "by every word that comes from the mouth of God."'" Then after scanning further, she read: "'We might well ask, "how could there be a personal relationship, a personal walk with God—or with anyone else—without individualized communication?"' We're not just supposed to talk *to* God, but also hear *from* God. That's how we walk in trust."

"I know where that's from," said Rob knowingly to Bridge.

"I know that my husband, Lyle, loves me, because he shows it to me. He tells me outright. He does things that communicate that he loves me. But he finds ways to let me know. God is doing that with us all the time, but if we never stop to figure out what he's saying, then sometimes we miss out on knowing—I mean, a deep knowing—that God loves us." As she said this, she pointed to her chest. "Even Jesus, with whom God was the most intimate, needed to hear God say that he loved him and was pleased with him. In Matthew, it's recorded twice."

But Stephen was in shock. "I'm not sure that I do that," he confessed. Then he backtracked, "I mean, I think I've heard God say things before. But is this supposed to be normal? Like, a usual thing? Is this the way it should be, all the time? Or how often? I don't think most Christians live like this."

"Isn't that the problem?" said Bridge. "What would you say if I said that I hadn't talked to Lyle in three months. Or more accurately, that I talked to Lyle, but didn't bother to listen to what he might have to say. What would you think of our relationship?"

"Dysfunctional," interjected Rob with a smirk.

"Right," as she turned to him. "We would think that something is wrong. But isn't it weird that when it comes to our *relationship* . . ." which she said by making quote fingers, "with God, that we don't expect to hear from him very much, if at all? We just read what he used to say, but we might not have much expectation that he might say something now."

"You believe this?" Stephen asked Rob. He was looking for some reassurance, but Bridge felt a little miffed by Stephen's need for backup.

He nodded. "It's in the Bible. That's what does it for me. Remember in John 10, Jesus said that the sheep will know the voice of the shepherd. He seemed to make it quite clear that we're all supposed to be able to recognize God's voice, if we are his. After tonight, I think she's really on to something."

"So if that's the case," said Bridge, making her point, "I think that's the aim for every believer. We should help every follower of Jesus to recognize God's voice in the everyday and obey what they hear."

With that, she wrote the word *recognize* in the diagram.

"If we push here, then it makes all of our disciplines make sense. Reading the Scriptures helps us know how God spoke in the past, so we can get a sense of how he might speak today. Memorizing Scripture becomes crucial, not just another notch in the spiritual belt. Prayer guides us to the space to have conversations—back and forth—with God.

"Community helps us discern, through the Holy Spirit. Other spiritual rhythms give us practice to have the power, through Jesus, to obey what we hear. All of this is like training to be a birdwatcher, remember? We're supposed to be God watchers. It also makes sense of the Bible, where people seem to talk to God with relative frequency. I'm not saying that we can conjure him up like Aladdin's genie, but if God is speaking to us, do we have ears to hear him? And then if we hear him, will we obey what we hear? When discipling someone, we're basically asking: what is God saying to you, and what will you do about it?

"And that's really important: we have to obey what we hear. At the end of the Sermon on the Mount, Jesus said that the difference between a person who can weather the storm and a person who can't is not in the rightness of a word, but rather if he puts it into practice or not. It's *not* in the quality of teaching, but in the quality of our obedience. That's the difference. Without obedience, then even a spot-on word from God will be worth nothing to us."

Stephen thought in silence.

If Rob was hesitant before, he now was on board: "I think it's what we need in our church to remind ourselves that Jesus is alive, he is active among us, and that we're not in charge. I guess I'm drinking the Kool-Aid. How do we get this into our church?"

Bridge punched Pastor Rob lightly on the shoulder and said with a smile, "It's about time."

CYCLE

The sun had already set, and the skies darkened quickly. Though the ocean breeze coming in through the windows was significantly cooler, it was still rather stuffy inside. The lights came on, and the room swelled with more people filling almost every chair both inside and on the outdoor patio near the sidewalk. The increasing volume of surrounding conversations made Stephen, Bridge and Rob lean in to hear each other better.

Bridge shifted the folio back in front of her and wrote another word at the bottom of the page: *hear.* "Here's how I think about training to hear God's voice," she said. "But it's also how I think about everything we do in the whole process of disciplemaking. We've just been talking about how to hear God's voice and how to discern it."

"Is this new?" asked Rob, pointing at the word *hear.*

She nodded. "I thought it would help clear things up more." Then she drew an arrow and wrote the word *respond.*

"But after we hear something from God, it moves us to respond in some way. It always presses us toward action. It can't stay in our heads. When we receive a new truth, it must change us in some way. What happens inside of us will play out in what we do. It has to. As James wrote, 'Faith without deeds is dead.' For James, it meant that if we say we love the poor, we will do something to meet their needs. What we do is important. Thinking, feeling and believing isn't enough."

"Building a house upon the rock," agreed Stephen.

"Right, we want people to respond to what they hear. To obey. So we've sown response into everything we do, whether it's our larger meetings or our Bible studies. Think about the high point, the climax, of a church service. What is it for most Protestants, particularly evangelicals?"

"The sermon," replied Stephen.

"Right. It's the about the word rightly preached. How about Catholics or more liturgical settings?"

"The Eucharist," said Rob.

"Exactly. The high point is to receive the sacrament, to receive grace you need for the week. What about charismatics?"

"Hm. I would guess either prayer ministry or worship," said Rob.

"I could buy that. I was thinking prayer ministry, but worship would be a great answer as well. Both are about visceral spiritual experiences, which is good. But what's the high point for Millennials? They're an action-minded group. They want to get in the thick of it, get their hands dirty, make a difference. I think the high point is the *response*."

Pastor Rob leaned back quickly. "Bridge, you've been holding out on me."

"Gotta come out more," she said with a grin. "So we've set up everything in our ministry to make sure that they always have a chance to respond to what they've heard or experienced. What will they do when they leave? And yes, they may experience some of the other things like a solid sermon and a spiritual experience. But all of that is a buildup to a practical response for what they will do after they leave. It could be a call to faith. It could be a call to action or service. But we always think of something that our students can respond to."

"We'd have to change our Sunday services to reach more young people," Rob replied.

"I think so," Bridge said. "And responding is really one of the few ways they can verify if God is speaking. If they hear something for a friend, then they can go up to that person and share what they heard. It's a risk, eh? But risk promotes trust. It promotes faith. You could say that without risk, what need would you have for trust? Our faith must act."

"But is that it?" asked Rob. "Sometimes they'll hear something and act correctly, but still things might not turn out the way they thought it would. Don't your students need help with that?"

Bridge sat silent for a moment. Stephen could see that she was stumped and that Rob had brought up a good point.

"What do you suggest?" Stephen asked Rob, trying to be helpful. The question seemed to jolt Bridge out of her thoughts.

Rob turned the folio toward him and took the pen out of Bridge's hand.

"Geez, Rob," said Bridge.

skeptic   seeker   follower
trust   challenge recognize
⟶

hear   respond
      ↓
  debrief

Rob mumbled an apology for taking the pen so abruptly but stared intensely at the page for a few moments before starting to draw another arrow and the word *debrief.*

"After they act," said Rob, "help them interpret what happened. That's important. You have to help them make sure they hear what God might want them to learn from this. Jesus does this with his disciples in Luke 10, where he praises their actions by saying that he saw Satan fall from heaven like lightning, and yet he gives them the correct perspective by asking them not to rejoice about the results of the ministry but that their names are written in the book of life. Jesus wants them to know that being in relationship with God is more important than what they accomplish."

"That seems important in recognizing God's voice," said Stephen. "We can get so caught up trying to hear a word from God that we forget to stay in relationship with him."

"That's good," said Bridge. "It's like the time Abraham hears God telling him to sacrifice his son. It's crystal clear. But ten short verses later, he tells him to stop. If he doesn't keep hearing God, then he'll miss the change in course. More than looking for an answer to a particular question, we are called to remain in him."

"Plus," said Stephen, "you can hear correctly, but the results could still be far from what you expected. Didn't Jesus say that if he was persecuted we would be also? Hearing God correctly could actually lead us into greater suffering."

"That's exactly what I'm talking about," said Rob. "We have to help them interpret things correctly. That's one reason why I came out. I wanted to see that it was guided well and kept within the biblical standards. I even gave an interpretation of Psalm 126 to help. Like I said, you did it well, Bridge."

Stephen thought he could see a slight blush coming from

Bridge's cheeks. Then he had an idea. *Should he . . .?* He reached for the pen.

"May I?" he asked, as he pulled the folio toward himself. Bridge nodded.

Stephen drew another arrow, connecting *debrief* and *hear.* He said, "All of this leads back to hearing God again. After you debrief, it'll help you discern how to hear God better the next time. It's a cycle!"

Rob smiled. "The circle is now complete," he said. "Well done, young *padawan.*" Stephen grinned.

Bridge sat silent for a moment. Then she admitted, "I hadn't seen that before. But when I think about it, it's exactly what we've been doing."

She looked up to visualize it more and slowly drew circles in the air with her finger. "If we keep this cycle up," she said, "then whenever we study Scripture, we know that it's not enough to learn the material, but we must hear God's voice through it. Then we press for response and debrief that response and see what God is saying through it. Then study some more to hear God's voice. Or with prayer. Or anything. If you keep this process in mind, you can develop disciples." She looked back and forth at both men when she said, "That's good stuff, guys."

"I wish I heard this months ago," said Stephen.

"It keeps us from allowing our discipleship to merely be in our heads," mused Rob. "Or on our butts in French cafés. Action is good for another reason: people remember far more from what they experience than from what they're taught. It's just a good way to teach."

"That's why Jesus had his disciples follow him for three years," Stephen said, as something clicked. "He wanted them not just to learn what he said, but to experience what he did and join in the ministry while he was still around. He was training them in word and action as you say, Bridge, 'to do what he did for the reasons he did them.'"

Bridge lit up with a huge smile. She loved that they were running with it on their own and was also glad to get a debrief of her own to make the model stronger.

REDUX

Bridge stared at the diagram for a moment. The pastries were long gone, mostly in Rob's stomach, and whatever was left of the coffee was cold.

"Hold on. Since we're already making some additions, let me add what we've been talking about. First, disciplemaking happens in *community* in each stage. A disciplemaker will find ways for a skeptic to trust the Christian community, then challenge them toward next steps within community, and then help a follower recognize God's voice and obey in community. It's clear that at any point of this diagram, the community is absolutely essential."

Then she wrote *the community of the Big Story* on top, with a couple of arrows:

"This process is about a person's story unfolding within a larger *communal* story. Jesus himself didn't think he could disciple one-on-one. He came from a tight community of three—Father, Son and Spirit—and then created another community of three—Peter, James and John. Then he had the Twelve, the seventy-two, the five hundred and the crowds. But he spent most of his time with the Twelve."

"Right," said Stephen, "I get that."

Bridge looked him in the eye as she dropped the bomb: "So, why are you discipling Jared one-on-one?"

He was caught. The entire time, he agreed with everything Bridge had to say about community, yet failed to apply that to his relationship with Jared. Busted, he just gave a sheepish smile and nodded his head.

"So I need to *respond*, don't I?" said Stephen. "But it's not like being on campus, or even at church. I'm not sure about how to do this with Jared. At work."

"What if coworkers got involved?" Rob chimed in.

Stephen's eyebrows furled at the thought. It felt like an overly simplistic answer coming from his pastor. After all, Rob had been a clergyman most of his working life. He had no idea how hard this would be at Stephen's workplace. Yet, he started to think about the people in his office for the first time. He felt some shame that he hadn't even thought about inviting others at work to what he was doing.

"I'll pray about it," Stephen said. After catching Bridge's suspicious glance, he said, "I'm not just saying that. I'll start praying for the people around me at work. Who knows, right?"

He surely didn't.

She seemed satisfied with that answer and wrote the words *Holy Spirit* on the page. "I might as well add this too. Look for the ways the Holy Spirit is moving around you at work. Your job is to be attentive. Put the antennae up and see if you can pick up on what God is doing at your workplace."

"Birdwatching," said Stephen.

"Who knows?" said Bridge. "God might actually surprise you."

PART 4

Leader

SHIFT

A few days after he talked with Bridge and Rob in the café, Darren knocked on the open door of Stephen's office. Darren worked in hardware, and he looked the part. His belly pushed against his short-sleeve button-down shirt, and neither his glasses nor his beard seemed straight on his face. But in his work, he was tough and exacting, which made him a particularly helpful engineer. Stephen supervised him now, even though Darren was at least a decade and a half his elder and had been at the firm during Stephen's entire tenure.

"Hey boss. I got a question for ya."

Stephen looked up, "Fire away."

"Why you hanging out with that kid so much?"

"Jared? Um . . ." Stephen was caught off guard by the question. *People are watching,* he thought. "He just wanted to pick my brain on a few things, and then he wanted to meet more regularly . . ."

"Every Tuesday?" he said with squinted eyes. "You and I have both been here a while, and you haven't taken this kind of interest in anyone. What's going on, boss?"

Stephen paused for a moment, debating whether he should come clean. Then, without consciously making a choice, he blurted out, "I'm mentoring him in his faith."

"Thought so," Darren grunted. Stephen expected him to turn on his heels and walk away, but Darren made Stephen's eyes go wide with his next words: "Can I join you guys?"

He went on to explain that he went to Mass on major holidays, but his wife was the devout one. But if they were going to do that at the office, he'd be interested. Then he quickly added, "If you'd let me."

Birdwatching, Stephen thought. He knew that Jared would be up for it, so he nodded and said with a smirk, "It looks like you already know when to meet."

Instead of getting back to work, he started fidgeting with a pen. If two people meeting caught the attention of the office, then three certainly would. He quickly shot up from his desk and headed over to Human Resources, straight for Sherrie's office. She was sitting at her desk, and her dark gray pantsuit and simple yet styled haircut all exuded professionalism.

"Hi, Sherrie. I don't actually have a problem with someone—for once." They both laughed. "I just have a question. Is it okay if I host a Bible study in my office during lunch on Tuesdays? No one is forced to come, but I wanted to know if it's okay with company policy."

"Let me talk to Terri about it," she said, referring to her supervisor.

It didn't sound promising to Stephen, but he didn't know what else he could do. So he offered his thanks and went back to his office.

A half hour later, he got another knock on his office door. He was surprised to see Sherrie standing in the doorway.

"That was fast," he said.

"She said it would be fine," Sherrie replied. "But don't play favorites. Promotions, raises, incentives—document your reasons and make sure everything is above board. Do that, and you'll be okay."

"Great, will do," he replied. "Thanks."

"One more thing," Sherrie added. "I want in."

Stephen tried to hide the shock on his face. He had no idea. She explained that she went to church on Sundays but would love to be a part of something like this at work. So she joined the group and increased their number to four. Without much intention from Stephen, the group doubled in a day.

START

At their first meeting, Stephen was the consummate host. In preparation, he had prayed each day for every person in the group and created a Bible study on John 1. He knew that they would bring bag lunches, but still, he had laid out bottled drinks and donuts on his desk to be hospitable. He had arranged the chairs in a circle, and on top of each was a printout of a Bible passage and discussion. He felt ready when he welcomed Jared, Darren and Sherrie into the room.

After Stephen's opening prayer, they introduced themselves, and Stephen learned something new about each person. He learned that Sherrie was a single mom whose daughter was already in college. He learned that Darren had been at the firm since it first began, ten years before Stephen's arrival. And that Jared's relationship with Karis, someone he'd met at church, had moved beyond merely dating and into a committed relationship.

"I didn't know about that," said Stephen, truly surprised.

"Just happened, dude," he said with a wide grin.

They went through the Bible study, Stephen leading all the way. He felt he had asked a great application question for a response: "In what ways do you think Jesus is asking you to 'come and see' at this point in your life?"

"I want to know if God can help me with my relationship with my daughter," said Sherrie, as her voice trembled. She shared openly about how their relationship fractured over time, so that now her daughter doesn't communicate with her at all. When tears started to well up in her eyes, Stephen was shocked. He had never seen Sherrie as anything else but strong and assertive, and here she was, in his office, as a daughter of God asking for help.

They prayed for Sherrie as tears fell down her face in silence. When they all said, "Amen," Sherrie didn't look up or around, but pulled out a tissue from her purse. "Who's next?" she said, stiffening her back.

Stephen looked in her eyes and said, "Thank you for trusting us."

She nodded, and after a moment of silence Jared startled the group by standing up from his chair.

"I know what I'm supposed to do," he said. "'Come and see' is for someone else too."

All eyes were on him, trying to decipher what he meant.

"I'm going to invite Casey to come next week," Jared said.

Both Sherrie and Darren looked questioningly at Stephen, and he didn't know how to respond. Casey worked in IT, and she was just a year or two older than Jared. And from previous conversations, Stephen felt sure that she was not a Christian. But before he could voice a possible objection about having Casey in the group, Jared had already left the room.

BABY

After a few weeks, preparing for each study became grueling for Stephen. He had to eke out times in the evening to get ready, which ate into his time with his family. He felt the weight of each person's personal struggles. Even small things like getting the refreshments and sending out reminder emails started to feel like a chore. He wasn't sure what to do, so he sent an email to a trusted friend.

Bridge offered to come up to Rancho Bernardo this time, so they met in his office during the lunch hour. He made good on his word and had sushi bento boxes waiting for the both of them. They dug in, sitting on opposite sides of his desk.

With chopsticks in hand, Stephen updated Bridge about the development of the group, enjoying the fact that they were in the room where much of the action had happened. He talked about his long hours of preparation, how responsible he felt in taking leadership, especially with more people to be concerned about. He wasn't just discipling Jared; now he was leading a whole community. And he was working harder than ever to attend to everybody's spiritual needs. "Do I get brownie points for each new person I take care of?" he asked. "It's bigger than just Jared now."

He waited for a commendation to leave Bridge's mouth, but instead she shook her head.

"Am I doing something wrong?" he asked, frustrated. He quickly looked at his clothes to see if anything was out of place or if he had spilled something on himself.

"You're babying him!" cried Bridge. "All of them!" She couldn't help herself.

"What do you mean?" said Stephen, a little defensively.

"I've seen this too many times before," said Bridge.

Stephen felt like he had placed his foot in a bear trap. His neck felt a bit hot, so he tugged at his collar.

"I thought—" he started, only to have Bridge wave him off.

"You can't be the only person giving to Jared or the group. You need to let them serve each other. If he's not ready to lead, at least give him something to do. Let him try on some responsibility for size, eh? Let them all do something to contribute."

Stephen tried to let the words sink in, but he thought she was being unfair. His group of two went to five, and he had done it exactly as she counseled. It had been a joy to watch them learn about Jesus and see them take steps to live out their faith. It felt a little out of place to be chastised. It was hard *not* to get annoyed.

"Bridge, you've been super helpful," he said slowly with a hint of condescension. "But aren't you being a little harsh?"

She paused and realized her agitation. She took a deep breath and said softly, "Sorry, Stephen. I was a little rough, eh? Let me back up. First, it's amazing what God is doing in your group. Seriously."

Stephen's shoulders relaxed a bit. "Man, I didn't know what I was doing wrong . . ."

"And you're also doing great things with Jared," she continued. "But if the group becomes about *you* meeting *their* needs, then it will ultimately fail. They'll become self-absorbed. You're not helping them. You're coddling them."

To blunt the blow, she added, "I learned this the hard way."

TRICKLE

Stephen felt the flow of air conditioning rush around him from the ceiling, trying to cool off his embarrassment. Bridge's eyes rolled up to the ceiling, retrieving the past from the recesses of her mind.

"When I first started off as a campus minister," she started in a tone that was oddly confessional, "we really wanted to welcome freshmen. So the upperclassmen hosted events, led small groups and basically served the freshmen all year. We thought that if you invested in them for a year, they'd turn it around and do the same for the class behind them."

That felt like a good plan to Stephen. What was wrong with that?

"But we realized that we were recruiting a certain kind of freshmen: ones who wanted to be coddled. Those with leadership gifts looked for places to exercise them, and when they couldn't find them in our fellowship, they left. We were left with the ones who wanted to be waited upon, as if they had nothing to contribute to the life of the faith community."

She paused to let that sink in. Stephen, after a moment's thought, started to realize that she might be right. He let his defenses down completely: perhaps a few decades in campus ministry might've given her *some* insight. He swallowed his pride and said, "Makes sense. What did you do instead?"

"Well, look at what Jesus did," she said, shifting closer to the edge of her seat. "When he invited people to follow him, what did he say? He said, 'Come, follow me, and I will send you out to fish for people.' From the beginning, he said that their lives would be in service to others. They would love God *and* love others, and they would be expected to contribute to the community straight away. Jesus was an expert leadership developer. That's exactly what we should be doing. We should be giving people the opportunity to lead as soon as possible. First, in small ways. Then later, when they have proven that they can handle it, in larger ways. We keep giving opportunities and thus develop them not only for their own souls, but for the mission as well."

"But doesn't the Bible say we shouldn't make people leaders too early?"

"Yes, but we're not talking about putting people in charge of everything. I'm using leadership in a more generic way: let them influence others. Give them responsibility that matches their maturity and giftedness."

Can't argue with that, he thought. After a moment's pause, he said: "It makes us—I mean, me—feel good to serve. I like it. And it's frankly easier to serve than to empower."

"You catch on quickly," said Bridge with a wink. "So to correct that, especially as we disciple someone, make sure they're contributing. Even Casey. For that to happen, you have to offer two things: power and authority."

"Come again?" asked Stephen.

POWER

Bridge pushed the empty Styrofoam bento boxes aside to make room for her familiar folio, which she placed on the desk.

She wrote the word *leader* in the next space of the arrow. "In Luke 9, when Jesus was sending out the Twelve into a short-term mission, it says that he gave them both *power* and *authority*. Both are needed. The first is power."

Stephen immediately had a gut reaction again the word *power*. He didn't trust it. He didn't want that many people to have it. And we definitely shouldn't be seeking it.

Bridge caught his reaction. "I keep forgetting you're an Xer. Yes, the talk of power is avoided in Christian circles, like we shouldn't have it. It's somehow dirty. And Christians have abused their power in the past, eh? We don't want to return to that. But it's come to the point that even if we bring up an imbalance of power within a Church community—like in conversations about race and gender—it's seen as a power play. It's a good thing the early church wasn't afraid of talking about it in Acts 6. But many of us think that being truly pious means to avoid power altogether."

"I definitely feel that," said Stephen.

"But that creates all kinds of problems. Lots of us think that we should shy away from the symbols of power, like higher education or large incomes. Some should, eh? But they're not, in and of themselves, at the heart of what's wrong. Those things are often needed to shape others, to be an influencer. In other words, to be a leader, you'll need to have some sort of power. Paul used his

Roman citizenship and top-notch education under Gamaliel to influence the world for Jesus. Without power, you won't get anything done. That's what power is: in the original language of the Bible, the word power is *dunamis,* where we get words like *dynamic* and *dynamite.* It's the ability to get things done."

Stephen still felt uncomfortable. "Isn't this the way Christians act in politics? But look where that got us."

"Yes, we don't want to abuse power. Or be corrupted by it. But let's think about it this way. I read that one form of power is the ability to successfully introduce a cultural good. So when we look up John 13, where Jesus washes his disciples' feet, it's the ultimate act of service. But it's also an exercise of a great deal of power."

Stephen wrinkled his eyebrows trying to follow along.

"He took a cultural rite, the washing of feet, and gave it meaning that is understood to this very day—two thousand years later. Its symbolism is not forgotten: it's about service. Jesus wanted us to remember, in the most absolute of terms, that as Christians, we are called to serve. He created a rite that would influence Christ followers for two millennia. If that's not influence and a good use of power, then I'd be hard pressed to find another."

Stephen thought about that for a moment. He had no problem with the connection to power and influence. But he had a harder time thinking that when Jesus was washing the disciples' feet it was an exercise of power. Was it really? It certainly was influential.

"But remember what the passage says right at the beginning?" asked Bridge. "It starts off with what Jesus knows. He knows that all things had been put under his power. He knows that he's the biggest dog in the pound. But Jesus does what is only reserved for the lowest slave. No Jewish slave would do it. Only Gentile slaves would. In a house with no slaves, everyone washed their own feet. The rite sticks, not because it was a slave who did the washing, but because someone powerful did. He used his power to create this cultural good that's still practiced to this day."

Power to serve? he asked himself.

"So, we are all called to exercise all the power we have, to serve and influence. But we are also called to lay down its cousin: *privilege.* Sometimes we blend the meanings of power and privilege, but there's a huge difference. Privilege is the *accumulation of benefits* that you receive from past successful uses of power. If we become influential, we will have racked up some privilege. And we're constantly called to lay it down. Use power, lay down privilege. That's servanthood."

This was blowing Stephen's mind way open: our higher education, our businesses, even our homes are helpful, because they are resources that can be used to serve others. Sure, we need to check our materialistic tendencies and to divest portions—or even all—of what we have. But we don't have to feel guilty about the things we've been given or need on a daily basis. They are resources we can use to serve. But we lay down privilege.

"Now that's not easy to do," she continued. "Using power can often feel like a struggle. We never have enough of it. We always find places where we are not able to get our way. So we want more and more power. And that idolatry of power will make us abuse our privilege as well. And when we get to a place where we are gaining privilege from our successful uses of power, we don't give that up easily. It's human nature, eh? You have to be on guard. Continue to wash feet."

"But there are other kinds of power in Scripture, right? Not just influence or resources. Like healing the sick. Casting out demons. Making the blind see."

"They're all resources," she said. "They're still ways for us to introduce a cultural good that might shape culture. If God used you to heal a woman from cancer, wouldn't that shape the soul of that survivor? When the power of God shows up, doesn't it shape a community's or organization's culture toward the kingdom of God? Doesn't Paul say that he wants to know the *power* of his resurrection, along with the fellowship of his suffering? Yes, both in the miraculous and the mundane, power is needed. And ultimately the Spirit is in us. He's a tremendous source of power for us, each and every day. But remember: we're also called to lay down privilege."

His mind was still chewing on this, but he wanted to keep on learning so he could synthesize this into a bigger picture. "So how does authority play into all of this?"

AUTHORITY

He glanced at his cell phone to check the time. They still had some left.

"If power is the ability or resource to do something," Bridge continued, "then authority is the *right* to do it. Authority in Jesus' day was the right or permission to rule, like over a province or a region."

"What does that mean today?"

"Everyone needs the permission to get something done. Particularly when you're a part of an organization, you can't just do you own thing. Your boss decides whether or not you're even allowed to do something. When you're at work, you can't do something that will be in direct opposition to your CEO, eh?"

"Absolutely," he said. He remembered when he said something critical about the leadership and the direction of the company. It bit him pretty hard in his review, and he was thankful not to have lost his job. Even if he was right, he didn't have the right to say it the way he did.

"But you need the opportunity to make your own decisions too, or else you'll feel like your job doesn't have much meaning."

He nodded. He hated the way his boss would overrule his decisions, sometimes arbitrarily. He unconsciously clenched his fist.

"It's the same in our churches," she continued. "They are organizations, after all. And like other organizations, we often give people either power or authority. But it's a rare thing to give them both. An organization that gives both is a healthier one.

But from where I am, you usually have one or the other. Ministries are often egregious in this area."

"What do you mean?"

"On the one hand, sometimes they give authority *without* power. That's a dangerous scenario. That's like giving someone charge over the youth group, but without any budget to buy the necessary materials, without any teachers to help move it along. We expect the leaders under us to make something happen, so we give them authority over a realm but don't offer any resources to back them up. We even forget to pray and bless them with spiritual resources to complete their tasks. We can really hang them out to dry. And they'll burn out."

Stephen had experienced this approach before. He was just a small group leader, but no one looked out for him. He was given a role with no mentor, no curriculum, but was expected to make something happen. It led not only to a quick burnout, but also to some bitterness against the ministry. He was wary to join any kind of leadership for a long time.

Stephen's eyes turned bright with realization. "As a manager, I would never let that happen at work. But at church, I not only let it happen, but I suffer through it too."

"Right. Power without authority is just as bad. We get them all excited about something and give them the necessary materials and resources, but we don't really let them lead. We're always involved, always correcting their decisions, always micromanaging. In the end, it not only stunts their growth, but they'll grow to resent us. They should have the authority to make their own decisions, and if they make a mistake, to learn from that along the way—so long as it doesn't tank the ministry. People, at almost every age, will need some sense of authority—the right to rule—in their given spheres of ministry. If we don't have that, then we'll get frustrated quickly or be so coddled that we'll never make our own decisions, and thus be stunted as leaders. That's a recipe for frustration."

He looked down: "That's what I'm doing with the Bible study. It's so weird, because I would never do that at work. I make sure that the vision is clear, that their roles are even clearer and that they have the resources they need to accomplish their tasks. That's just good management."

"Exactly. Everyone, no matter how low they are on the organizational chart, wants to exercise power and authority. They're wired to. Even if they have a small budget and a tiny realm, at least they are making decisions and have the power to influence that area. Employees who have this are among the highest in job satisfaction. But in ministry, when pay is low and status often lower, it becomes more imperative that the role itself is life-giving. Jesus knew this better than anyone else, and he gave Christians *his* authority."

"Management skills and ministry coming together?" he said jokingly. "Who knew that it would be possible on this side of heaven?"

"But giving authority doesn't mean that you just toss your authority away. Don't confuse eagerness for competence. If they're under you, they're going to need your guidance, and if they're heading down the wrong path, you wouldn't be a good leader if you didn't offer correction. It's just another way of giving more *power:* resources to fulfill their role. And they're going to need your guidance, so don't just do the classic management mistake of letting them run completely on their own. It's easy to do, especially if they are high performers. Always keep them connected to what you think God is calling the group or organization to do. Remember the circle? Debrief."

"I'm glad you said that," he said. "I probably would've just let them run with it."

"Right, it's hard to keep a good balance between correction and micromanaging. That's where discernment is helpful, and getting advice and wisdom from other leaders will help you along here."

"Seems like you've mastered it."

"Not even close. I'm tweaking it all the time. But that's why the students are leading the charge in the response on campus, but I'm also there making sure they don't fail. I want to help them succeed, but they need to be coming up with the ideas and taking the risks. See, I'm giving them power and authority. At this stage, you're empowering."

And she wrote down the word *empower* on her folio:

"And remember to apply the hear-respond-debrief cycle you helped to create."

She's empowering me, he thought. He wouldn't forget.

CUT

At the following week's Bible study, Stephen couldn't wait to tell them what he had learned and that they were changing the format to take turns leading.

It was nearing lunchtime, and Stephen was tidying up his desk a bit before the others arrived. Jared stepped into his office first, with a huge smile. He grabbed one of the folding chairs from where it was leaning against the wall, flipped it out and plunked down.

"How's Karis?" Stephen asked.

Jared didn't say anything at first. He just grinned so wide that there was enough room for all of his teeth to jump out. He didn't know that he would be dropping a bomb in this office.

"Over the weekend, she invited me to move in with her. So it's happening. I'm moving in on Friday."

Stephen immediately froze. He looked up and asked the best clarifying question he could come up with: "What?"

"Yeah, things are going so well that she invited me to move in. We can spend more time together, and I can save some money . . ."

"But don't you think that's a bad idea?" started Stephen.

"Nope. It'll be a great way to . . . oh?" he started to smirk. "I see what you're getting at. Dude, nothing's going to happen. We're both Christians. We both love God. It's going to be alright."

"But it's not going to look good."

"No one blinks about it these days."

"But you guys are going out."

"Don't worry, dude. *Nothing's* gonna happen."

Stephen knew that he was pushing now, but he couldn't let it go. "But sometimes things get out of control, you know? Seriously, you should think more about it."

"It's a done deal," he smiled. He had a way of turning on the charm when things weren't going his way. "Seriously, you can trust me on this one."

Stephen felt stuck and let the silence creep into the room. He clearly wasn't getting anywhere, but he knew that this wasn't a good idea. He was trying to figure out what to say next when Darren entered the room.

"Darren," said Stephen. "Jared and I disagree about something." He turned to Jared and asked, "Is it okay if I share it with him?"

"Sure," he said.

"Jared, why don't you tell him what's going on?" said Stephen, with a change of mind. He didn't want to unfairly bias the story.

Casey and Sherrie walked into the office at the same time. It took just one glance at the others in the room to make them drop their smiles.

"What's going on?" Sherrie asked.

"I was just about to tell Darren that I'm moving in with Karis on Friday."

No one said anything for a little bit. Casey was the first to break the silence: "Are you sure that's a good idea?"

"Seriously?" he asked, now crossing his arms and his charm fading. He was surprised that it came out of Casey's mouth instead of the others.

Darren added, "I might be a bit old-fashioned, but don't you want to wait to do something like that? Sharing that kind of intimacy without a promise to stay together, well, that's a bit like having a swelling river with no banks. It's not a river anymore. It's a flood."

Stephen remained silent. Sherrie went next in her kindest voice, "I don't have to tell you my story again to talk you out of this, do I?"

Sherrie's comment broke through his defenses. He lowered his shoulders and his arms and asked another question: "Casey, why don't you think it's a good idea?" He really thought she'd be cool with it.

She looked up and shuffled her feet a bit. She was clearly thinking of what to say next. Then, in a soft voice, she said, "Because, well, you're a *Christian.*" Her voice lingered over the last word, and she didn't know what else to say.

If Sherrie's comment brought down his defenses, then Casey's was an arrow to the heart. Or more like a surgeon's scalpel. He didn't quite understand it all, but if *she* thought that moving in with Karis wasn't compatible with being a Christian, then he'd at least have to think about it more.

All eyes were on Jared. He looked at everyone and the concern in their eyes reminded him that each one of them loved him deeply. He knew this community only wanted good things for him. So he shrugged and then shook his head while he stared at the floor.

"I hear you guys," he said, without looking up. "I'm not just saying that. I'll talk to Karis about it, and I'll get back to you."

Then in another moment, though still a bit bruised inside, he smiled a huge grin while clapping his hands and said loudly, "Alright, Stephen. What you got for us?" And after they each gave him a hug, they sat down and opened their Bibles.

SKIN

To prepare for the next study, Jared came over to Stephen's house after they both had another late night at work. The kids were already sleeping, so they sat at the dining table in his kitchen. Stephen was glad to hear that Jared wouldn't be moving in to Karis's place, and they talked about what would happen at the next Bible study. Jared was excited to teach. He'd be the first to lead the new study on Matthew that Bridge had suggested.

"What do you think of this genealogy?" asked Stephen about Matthew 1.

"Just a bunch of names," Jared replied.

"Anything stand out?"

Jared pored over the names. "There are four women. Tamar, Rahab, Ruth, Mary. Four women in a list of men. What does that mean?"

"Lists like these, back then, wouldn't even mention the women."

"So Jesus welcomes the *ladies,*" he winked. "I like that."

"That's just nasty, man!" Stephen choked out through his laughter.

"I'm just playin'. Okay, women are included."

"Can you tell me about each of them?"

Jared pulled out his phone, and Stephen was about to stop him. At first, that felt like cheating. But isn't this a great way for Jared to find information for himself? So he let the search continue.

"Whoa," said Jared, talking as he scrolled through pages. "Tamar tricked her father-in-law into sleeping with her to have a baby. Rahab was a prostitute from Jericho. Ruth, from Moab, basically seduced Boaz, though he had the right to be with her." Then he looked up: "And I know Mary: a virgin who was also pregnant."

"So what does that mean?"

Jared took a moment before responding, "Those who were on the outside are now in. Outcasts are welcome. If you were born as a woman in a man's world, or a Gentile in an Israelite world, or you just had hard times—you can still be connected to Jesus."

"You'd make a great preacher, man." Stephen smiled. He could feel pride welling in his chest.

But Jared stared at the back of his hands for a long while, lost in thought. Then he said slowly, "I'm on the outside, dude." He paused more, looking Stephen in the eyes, wondering if he could share these thoughts with his spiritual mentor. It felt more weighty given Jared's general impulsiveness.

Taking Stephen's silence as encouragement, he started to talk. He showed Stephen the back of his hands: "I'm not white. In this country, that means something."

Stephen unconsciously looked down at his own hands. His shoulders and neck reflexively tensed at the mention of race. He swallowed hard, wondering not only where this was coming from, but also what maelstrom of feelings might erupt before him. Jared, however, was more subdued.

"But I'm not clear what I am," he said. "I'm a quarter African-American, and a quarter Asian through my adopted half-Korean mom, and a quarter Caucasian and a quarter Latino—British and Mexican, to be exact. When people look at me, they try to put me in some category, some box. I don't have a community to call my own."

Stephen thought that Jared would start to tear up. But when he looked up to see, Jared's eyes were dry, almost vacant. He spoke of a reality that he was already tired of.

"I'd like to belong," said Jared. "But where would I go? I can't pass as white. Latino or Filipino could work. East Asians won't accept me as one of their own. And I'm evenly split between them all. Should I go to the people I look most like?"

Stephen didn't know what to say. He was listening intently, nodding in empathy. The riddle of Jared's ethnic background had finally been solved, but it also now brought up many more questions of its own. In the ensuing silence, Stephen stayed with the topic at hand and asked a question: "Why do you have to choose?"

"Dude, exactly. But if I don't choose, I'm homeless. Who are my people? Where do I belong? Do I dabble in it all, like some racial buffet? Do I just taste a little bit of each? That's me, none of the above. Checking all that apply." He swished his hand in the air, checking off an imaginary census form.

Stephen didn't have much of an answer. He thought they were going to talk about his faith. He wasn't prepared to go here. And he didn't want to say something that would be offensive. As he deliberated, he suddenly jerked his head up sharply in realization and started to speak.

"I know this is hard, but I'm glad you're talking about it," Stephen said. "I don't have to think about it. I'm white. I have the luxury of *not* thinking about it. Just like I don't have to think about being a man. Or straight, for that matter. Being in privilege means that I don't have to think about things. And so I can divorce my ethnic identity from my faith. But I shouldn't. And I'm glad that you're not. We do have to talk about it. I mean, it showed up in our Bible study, right?"

Jared looked up in bewilderment. Then he smiled. He didn't expect Stephen to say something like that, but he was glad he did. It allowed him to relax, and he felt free to talk about his ethnicity without fear of offending his mentor. He let out a sigh.

"Did you know that racial categories—the stuff we use every day like white, black or Asian—are just made up?" Jared said excitedly. "I just saw this video where it goes through the history of race. Back in the late 1700s, in Jefferson's time, people didn't even categorize people by race. Identity was usually by status, wealth or culture. But people didn't think of themselves as 'white.' It's hard to even grasp that idea now, right?"

Stephen nodded, because he had to admit it was.

"But greed fueled racism," he continued, the intensity of his voice rising with each sentence. "Plantation owners needed African slave labor to keep their businesses running. The government wanted to expand America to the Pacific, and what better way to unify both rich and poor whites than with a message of superiority? That way, if the first peoples of this land were less valuable, then their land could be taken. Even scientists backed up these racial differences, ones that we know aren't true today. Race was made up to put others down. And now it haunts me today, forcing me to choose," Jared's fists clenched and his voice rang with a greater intensity. "Why should I keep contributing to something so messed up?"

Even though he knew to just listen, Stephen still felt a shroud of guilt when the conversation turned to race and ethnicity. He felt helpless. He didn't create this mess. His ancestors did. But he also knew that he benefitted from these past injustices. He lived in a stolen country. Still, he felt blamed. At times, he'd have to fight against anger, feeling that lists like these always made him the bad guy. It took some effort to keep concentrating on what Jared was saying, but he also knew enough to just listen.

"So I gave up," Jared said. "Why try? It's too much work. How would I identify with the four different streams with the same kind of heart? Why should I have to work four times as hard as everybody else! I want to choose American, but some of my bloodlines have been here for centuries, and we're still not treated as full Americans. It's not that some of us crossed the border, but that the border crossed us!"

Stephen's eyes were wide open. The last sentence had more implications than just ethnic identity. Paralyzed, he shot up a prayer in his mind: *help!*

PRIVILEGE

Bridge propped her elbows up on the table for a moment, cupping her latte. The afternoon sun streamed in through the glass walls on the long line of people waiting to purchase their much-needed octane for the rest of the day. She stared out at the campus's graduate housing across the street and wondered momentarily how living on campus could help with her ministry.

She caught him waiting for her and quickly gathered her thoughts. "Well, of course he did," she said to Stephen. He had explained his surprise over the last conversation with Jared on ethnic identity and his paralysis over the political implications. She gave her gut response, but then she realized that she might have to mull it over to have it make sense to him. "Forget the politics for now. But let's start at the beginning. Ethnic identity is a valid biblical identity marker," she started to say. But before she could finish her thought, he cut in.

"You don't have to go there," he said, waving his hands in protest. "I know. White is an ethnic identity. And I know that being white comes with some privileges in this country. I know that I can use my privilege to bless others—to use my power to influence, but to lay down privilege for those who don't have the same access. And I know I don't have to feel guilty either, though it's not easy. I get that."

Bridge let her shoulders fall to relax. She already had a lot to deal with, just being a woman in Christian ministry. She didn't want to have a tough conversation about ethnicity as well. "Looks like you connected the dots from our last conversation."

He nodded. "So what would *you* do for someone like Jared? Sure, I'm multiracial. But I can still come under one banner: white. He doesn't have that luxury. He has to think about it as someone who isn't white in this country, so it's way more complex. He doesn't know where he should go with it or how it fits into his faith."

"But if you buy that ethnic identity is important in faith, that's most of it," said Bridge. "We can work from there. First, his utmost identity is in Jesus. His primary identity is a child of the King, a co-heir with Christ. In that, he can rejoice."

"Right, nothing trumps that." Stephen knew she would say that, but still felt relieved at the comment.

"Knowing that, then, he can rest in the full knowledge that Jesus didn't mess up when he made him. There was a purpose and a reason. And he could explore what a multiracial identity in this country feels like in that security. Plus, the number of multiracial people in this country is climbing quickly. You can now check 'multiracial' on the census. So encourage him to learn, at his own pace, about the different cultures that make up who he is. But he might also be a new kind of American, with a varied ethnic past, and *that* could inform his future."

"A new kind of American?"

"Sure, one that isn't just vested in merely white interest. Or in any one particular group's interest for that matter. One that might be freer to use its power and privilege to bless people who are not like them. Isn't that what loving our neighbors is about?"

"But why does that matter for faith?"

"Embracing it will help us to cross cultures and subcultures more effectively. Ignoring it means that we're blind to the ways we, as a group, might potentially sin against others, which will affect our credibility as witnesses."

Stephen just shook his head and then dropped it into his hands. Bridge realized that this probably wasn't helping.

"Let me try again," she said. "Why are we given ethnic identities?"

Stephen just looked up, blinking. "This is supposed to help?"

"Seriously. Think about that. If we believe that everything has been given to us to be a blessing to others—another form of *power*—then what is it about ethnic identity that is a blessing? Too much of ethnic identity talk is self-centered. We make it about inner healing or claiming something that helps us belong. But this is really just the starting point. It's supposed to lead to something."

"Go on," he said, more leerily than he wanted to show.

"Our ethnic identity isn't just about us. It's meant to bless. That's how all things are in the kingdom. So when we think about it, Jared has a few things that he can do with his brown multiracial identity—though it's not about race. It's about ethnicity. It's about culture. First, he can identify with other brown multiracial people. Second, he can always claim one part of his identity to connect with others. So if he ever gets turned on for the mission, he could speak on behalf of each of the communities that are inside of him."

Stephen thought this line of reasoning was intriguing. "He could make tons of connections."

"Right, and with those connections, he could speak on behalf of those communities and be an agent of reconciliation. He could even talk about the reconciliation that occurred in himself, with the races mixed, to talk about the integration of these things—that in him, reconciliation to some extent is happening, and it is a foretelling of what is to come. One day, we will all be reconciled. One day, every tribe, nation, language and tongue will worship before the throne."

Stephen had to think about that for a moment. Not only could

Jared connect with a bunch of different communities and bridge them, but he can also speak of an integration that is to come, foretold in his different bloodlines.

"Then, he can speak of the two becoming one in himself and how he longs for that in the larger body. But that isn't all of it. On the other hand, with the dissonance of not being able to connect to anyone, he can speak of his experience as a sojourner in the land. As a follower of Christ, he knows what it means to be a sojourner, to long for home one day. That ache to belong will find its fulfillment in the end. All things are redeemable."

Bridge sounded so passionate and so excited; it was hard not to be caught up in the moment. Still, he knew that even though these things were possibly redemptive, it would still be hard. And that Jared's road is one that is particularly unique.

"But he's still got it hard."

"No doubt. But much of his life can be a pointer to Jesus and a foretelling of the reconciliation to come. In the meantime, there are other multiracials who are going through a similar experience in finding themselves between ethnicities and cultures, though from different contexts. Connecting with other multiracials, particularly Christians, could be powerful."

Stephen paused to let this sink in, and yet the lines across his forehead betrayed his worry. He didn't feel like he wasn't the one to have this conversation with Jared, but he was worried it would come off as a cop out.

"Would *you* mind bringing this stuff up to Jared?" he asked tentatively.

"Feeling too white for the job?" she grinned.

He laughed awkwardly but was gladder still when she agreed.

PART 5

World Changer

ALTAR

The new structure for the Mobiship Bible study seemed to go well. Stephen was glad to see the ways each of them were taking risks to lead. They each had a different style: Jared, of course, loved to tell stories. Darren would make them dive deep into the text. Sherrie would help them relate to the passage by uncovering underlying motivations of the biblical characters involved.

Casey, however, was a delight. She wasn't yet a believer, but she led times that were honest. She'd ask the question that *should* be asked but no one else was asking. When she led out of Matthew 5:21-26, she asked if Christians *really* try to reconcile with people who are angry with them before they go to church on Sundays? She saw the Scriptures with new eyes, and it made everyone apply a passage they may have overlooked.

As well as the studies were going, Stephen was more grateful for the one-on-one times he started to have on Fridays during lunch. Even though they met to talk about the upcoming Bible study, other things—more personal things—would often come up. Like last time:

"So this part of the Bible says I should reconcile with people who are angry with me, right?" asked Casey.

"That's what it says."

She paused a bit before blurting out: "Maybe I need to talk with Sherrie."

Perplexed, Stephen fell silent for a moment. He hadn't seen anything of a conflict brewing between them. Sure, he'd noticed that Casey was a little self-conscious about not being a Christian in the group, but he honestly thought that she was feeling more and more comfortable. He was genuinely surprised.

"Why do you think she has something against you?" he asked.

"She's a little *cool* to me."

Stephen didn't want to start an interrogation, but it felt like a vague answer. He really wanted to know what was going on.

"Did something happen?" he asked.

"Sort of. I mean, she's mostly fine in the group. At least, I didn't sense it as much there. But when we would run into each other in the hallway, she doesn't say more than a sentence or two. I feel like she's blowing me off, and even in our meetings she seems a little more critical with me than the others. I don't know. Maybe I should just drop it . . ."

"Maybe," said Stephen. "But you *are* feeling something here. Let's try to figure out what's going on." Stephen knew Sherrie could come off a little strong at times. But without much else to go on, he felt a little lost. "Have you brought it up with her?" he asked.

"No, not really. I used to visit her once in a while, but when I felt like she kept blowing me off, I stopped going."

"Maybe you could . . ."

"What do you think she'll say?"

"I don't know. But you won't know unless you talk to her."

"I know," she said more quietly. But her eyes were like daggers. "It's unfair, ya know? I'm the one trying to learn here. She's the Christian! I'm not. She's the one acting like a . . ." She stopped herself.

In the growing silence, he lifted a silent prayer.

DEBT

Stephen was torn. He knew what he'd say to a Christian: Forgive as you have been forgiven. Talk to the person and find out what's going on. But with Casey, he felt a lot more cautious. *How much do I hold her to, as someone who's not a Christian?*

But he also knew that she trusted him. He could hear Bridge in his head calling him to *challenge* her to the next step. If God's truth was actually truth for everyone, then he'd have to address this as if Jesus' words were true for everyone: that forgiveness is really at the heart of the good news, and that we can be a part of a healing movement because of what God has done for us. He took a deep breath and jumped in.

"Let me put this in the bigger picture. This is what I've been learning from a friend of mine. In the Christian story, we are secret agents of a huge covert operation of God, who wants to heal the world and everyone in it. It happens this way: Jesus restores us so that we can be a source of healing to others."

"Okay," she said, not really knowing where this was going.

"A major part of the story is that we are forgiven by God. Jesus dies with the junk in our lives, taking the power of sin and death down to the grave with him. But he comes back to life three days later to show us that sin and death don't get the final say. A new life is possible. A new world is available."

"Yeah, that's what we've been talking about." She crossed her arms, impatiently.

"So, you're being invited to die with Jesus when it comes to

Sherrie. Right now, you feel wronged by her. Whether she did it intentionally or not, we don't know. But you feel it. So you're being invited to die to your need for revenge, retribution or whatever you feel like she owes you. But in Jesus, you have the power to forgive her. You forgive her, because Jesus forgave you. She doesn't owe you anything: her debts are paid. In this, you're being invited to life in Jesus' resurrection, living restored to her. You get the privilege to clear things up with her, to find out what's going on. Jesus forgave you. You forgive her in your heart and then you seek restoration."

"What if she doesn't listen to me? What if she doesn't understand?"

"That's not up to you. What's up to you is to forgive as Jesus forgave you. Then seek restoration as much as possible. If it doesn't work out, then you've been faithful to try. You may try again later, but you can't force her to do anything. Then you'll find ways to cope while still continuing to hold her in love. Definitely don't put yourself in a situation to get burned over and over, but you're still called to forgive. What would Jesus ask you to do?"

"What do you mean? Remember, I'm not the Christian here."

Still, Stephen pressed in: "Don't let that be an excuse. I think you know."

After a brief pause she said, "Jesus would ask me to talk to Sherrie."

He smiled warmly. "It's way easier to ignore her. But God actually wants you both to experience something even more profound—that relationships can be healed, that you can live in a new kind of world, where people forgive. It sounds like God is trying to get your attention."

She paused. All of it made sense to her, but she had never done anything like this before. She really did just avoid people after feeling burned. But this time something tugged within, and she knew what she had to do. Resolve set in.

"Okay, I'm in," she said, hesitation disappearing.

"Can I pray for you?"

ISSUE

After they prayed, Stephen knew that Casey would be heading directly to Sherrie's desk. So he picked up the phone and gave Sherrie a call.

"Hey, you busy?" asked Stephen.

"Um, we're both at work," she deadpanned.

"I know!" he laughed. "But I want to give you a heads up. Casey's coming to your desk right now." He then explained briefly that Casey felt like Sherrie was being cold to her and that she was going over there to restore the relationship.

"I know that you're in HR, and so you're probably already good at this. But I just wanted to give you heads up so you can hear her out. You okay with that?"

She paused, and at that moment Stephen wished he could see her face instead of being stuck on the phone. He had no idea how she'd react, and he started to get worried. But what she said startled him: "Dang, it's my issue. She's just so much like my daughter—" Then she cut herself off, and after a few seconds ticked by, said, "I didn't know that it was affecting her. Thanks for the heads up. I see her coming."

"Okay, let me know how it goes."

"I will." And she hung up.

Stephen spun around in his chair and prayed again.

BLOOM

Bridge looked up at the stars while the worship band continued to play. The music felt a bit like someone kept changing the radio station, because one song would come from Hillsong, but the very next one would come from Kirk Franklin. But as they worshiped in different cultural styles in the Price Center courtyard, it was healing.

Bridge's heart felt full watching her Asian and white students worshiping together with the black and Latino students from other campus communities. One of the black students introduced the night, saying: "UCSD was known as a racist campus. Look around you, do you see racism here this evening? No. UCSD Campus Ministries has taught me how to love, and it's a beautiful thing." With those words, Bridge remembered the image of the river from the student leaders' meeting a month ago. Tears flowed down her cheeks.

Rallies had happened every day since the first protests. After that meeting in a church's upstairs room, her students had decided to go to the next big one. Everyone from Campus Ministries wore an armband with the word *pray* written on it. She had no idea that more than three hundred of her students would come. Their presence was felt. One student at that rally actually said, "I walked away from the church because I thought God doesn't care about justice . . . [but] today I look at all of you here, and I know that we are sisters, we are family. God really does care about this." Another black student said that there were only two places where he felt safe on campus: BSU and UCSD Campus Ministries. It was a glorious sight to see. Bridge couldn't have been prouder.

The students had also urged Bridge to lead a talk series on multiethnicity to give the entire group a sense of what God is doing on their campus and what the gospel might say to it. On top of it all, after Campus Ministry's involvement in the rallies, the campus administration had sought them out to provide cross-cultural training for every new fraternity and sorority pledge.

As Bridge looked around, she caught a glimpse of someone at the back of the gathering. Where most people were standing, he was leaning back low in his chair, with his arms crossed. She tried to make eye contact, but he kept looking down with a hood pulled over his brow. She started toward him, but after she took only a few steps, he bolted straight up and walked briskly in the other direction.

In a few moments, Jared was out of sight.

GIFT

After the UCSD worship event, Bridge and Stephen sat at a café on campus yet again to talk about Jared's spiritual development. It was nestled in a corner of the Price Center and had seating both indoors and out. They sat outside, enjoying the spring sunshine and the cooling ocean breeze that flowed through the campus. She explained all that happened in the past month and a half. Then she pulled out her folio.

"We're at the last stage," she said. "Now that they've shown some leadership in the Christian community, they're also supposed to influence the world around them. It can't be about merely blessing insiders. We should also seek to bless outsiders. Be salt and light."

"Yeah, we just studied that in our group. I wish we were better at it."

"No doubt. So in disciplemaking, we also want them to become world changers." With that, she wrote *world changers* near the end of the arrow. "No one can change the whole world. Only God can do that. But we can each affect the world around us. In that way, we are world changers."

"I like how discipleship isn't just about us."

"Right, and our culture has become very polarized: Red vs. Blue, gay vs. straight, atheist vs. religious, Fox vs. CNN, rich vs. poor. In almost every public arena, we are fighting each other with more venom and vengeance. We can't get along with people who don't look like us or who think differently than us. Even our government can't seem to work together across the aisle for helpful solutions. And as we saw on campus, we can't even get along in the university. I think that's a major problem in culture today: we have no idea how to reconcile. We just fight to have our own way."

Stephen's mind drifted toward the news headlines of the day. He couldn't remember living through a more contentious time in the public square.

"Given this climate, I think racial issues will become much harder to work through as well. Our culture has lots of words for trying to get along, like diversity, tolerance, political correctness, equal rights or access. They're all just ways of putting up with each other, so we don't offend anyone. Reconciliation is so much harder, though. It's not just about putting up with each other, but actually living rightly with each other in *shalom,* in love and justice. We'd have *rightness* in our relationships."

"Everything would be made right," he said, almost wistfully.

"To reconcile, you start with forgiveness. You have to admit that something wrong was done. But acknowledging wrong requires a standard of right and wrong, of good and evil, and that's missing in our postmodern world. And even if you admit evil has been done, you then have to forgive. That's not a grasping for rights, but a laying down of perceived rights to heal the whole. Then it must be made right again: justice occurs, restoring things to the way they're supposed to be. In these three things—acknowledging wrong, forgiving and restoring—reconciliation occurs. Who else should be better equipped to forgive and restore relationships?"

Stephen could already smell the implications of what she was saying. "So you're saying that Christians could offer the gift of reconciliation in our culture?"

"Exactly. That's one unique offering in a time of great need. It's at the heart of the Christian message. Paul sums up his ministry with that word: *reconciliation,*" said Bridge. "In 2 Corinthians 5, he speaks of a reconciliation between God and mankind. But in other parts of Paul's writings, like in Ephesians 2, God reconciles us to each other as well, because we are already reconciled to God. It's our way to love God and love others. The abolitionist movement and the civil rights movement were spearheaded by Jesus-followers. I think that our ability to reconcile estranged people and communities on this side of heaven will validate the truth that we are also reconciled on the other side."

"But I don't think we're very good at that either."

"Fair enough. But that is what God is doing in the world, with everything. One of my favorite texts is Colossians 1:15-20. It says that all things, under heaven and on earth, are reconciled back to God through his blood shed on the cross. All things. Do you know what that means?"

"All things?" he said flatly.

She shook her head. "But do you get it? It means that everything can be reconciled. Not just my relationship to God, and not just yours. But also our relationships to each other. And the ways we relate to the wider world. Even our culture can be redeemed. It's powerful: arts, music, movies, anything that we might think is completely depraved can find its way to be redeemed again. All of these things can be put back to right. A new world is possible. So there are many possibilities about how our discipleship can bless beyond the walls of our own church. The point is that we have to give people a big enough vision to bless the people around us, not just fellow believers. We need to cast vision for broader impact."

She then wrote the word *envision* in the diagram, underneath *world changer:*

skeptic   seeker   follower   leader   world changer
trust   challenge   recognize   empower   envision

"How do we do that?" asked Stephen.

CALL

Here's a little equation I use." And she flipped the page and drew and arrow and wrote the word *calling:*

$$\longrightarrow \quad \textit{calling}$$

"Really? Another diagram?" he mocked. "Such a Boomer."

"But they help, eh?" she said, without pausing. "I think we're ultimately helping disciples discern their calling in this life. I think of it as a deep-seated conviction from God about what each person is uniquely meant to bring to the world. Only God can give you that, which is why it's so vital to learn how to recognize God's voice in the context of his community."

"I'm following," he said.

"Two things inform this calling, but don't necessarily lock us in. That's why it's an arrow instead of an equal sign. The first is our gifting." Then she wrote the word *gifts* nearer the left-hand side of the page:

$$\textit{gifts} \qquad \qquad \longrightarrow \quad \textit{calling}$$

"There are plenty of assessments available to help people understand their gifts or strengths. But you're basically trying to identify, in cooperation with the Holy Spirit and feedback from the Christian community, what someone's gifts might possibly be. In Scripture, spiritual gifts are God-given talents that are meant to bless the common good. That's an important distinction. Our gifts come from God, whether we acknowledge it or not. But the way we use our spiritual gifts is meant for the common good and not for our own glory."

"I think that's a helpful word for the Millennials. It keeps it from being a narcissistic quest."

"The other thing that informs our calling is our passions." With that, she wrote a plus sign and the word *passions:*

$$gifts + passions \longrightarrow calling$$

"Frederick Buechner wrote that 'The place God calls you to is where your deep gladness and the world's deep hunger meet.' The Latin root for our word *vocation* means 'to call.' Our work, regardless of where it shows up on the status scale in our culture, should reverberate with a sense of call."

"What if we don't know what we're passionate about?" he asked. He wasn't thinking of Jared at this point.

"That's what disciplemakers should help with," she continued. "They can't tell people what to do. But they can ask questions, offer advice, pray and help discern God's voice with a disciple. The disciplemaker helps point out what might potentially be gifts and passions. But we don't force our opinions on them. They'll have to figure it out in the end, with the guidance of God's Spirit, of course. Basically, we help them answer this question: what would the kingdom of God look like if it showed up around you?"

"Any examples?" he asked. He hoped she would say something that would inspire him.

WORK

Bridge looked around the campus, searching for inspiration. It wasn't that she couldn't think of anything. Quite the opposite.

"So many to choose from," Bridge said. "The range could be the lawyer who is fighting for justice in his spare time, or the janitor who scrubs as if God will be visiting. Perhaps a dentist who not only serves his wealthier clients but also gives a portion of his time to those who can't afford dental care or a policy maker who seeks justice. It could be the full-time minister who is preaching from the pulpit each Sunday, or the athlete who gives God glory through excellence and character, or the stay-at-home husband who devotes himself to the spiritual nurture of his children. Some people are called overseas to use their skills in the poorest slum areas of the world, while others serve in the rarified halls of governmental powers. Perhaps one can write Hollywood scripts infused with kingdom values, while another writes worship songs sung by churches throughout the world. Each person has unique gifts and passions that can contribute to a sense of calling. No person can change the *entire* world. That's God's job. But each person can be a world changer."

"I'm glad you didn't say to just be a missionary."

"Well," she replied. "If you mean giving up all of your possessions and flying to Africa, then I would say, 'Not necessarily.' But never say 'never.' You're right, though. Not everyone is even called to be clergy. But if you mean that everyone is called to be a witness wherever they are, then I'd say, 'Absolutely.'"

"But isn't full-time ministry the highest calling?" he asked. He meant it. It seemed like the high bar of being a Christian was being clergy. The laity felt like second-class citizens in the church.

"It depends what you mean. We are all in ministry. The Bible says we're all priests. But that doesn't mean we all work in a ministry organization. But since we spend so much time at work, shouldn't we find ways to worship while at work? Can the work itself be redeemed, or was it meant to all be thorns, thistles and toil?"

He yearned for redeemable work. He wasn't sure it was at Mobiship.

"One example is of a Harvard-educated computer engineer who then became a campus minister for some years. Then he realized he wanted to be back in the business sector and now co-owns a company that trains young people who were orphaned by the Rwandan genocide to make greeting cards—high-quality stuff that's sold at market prices. Not only are they offering well-paying jobs in one of the poorest countries in the world, but they also offer training so that these workers can eventually start their own companies."

Nonprofits, he thought. "Sure, but what about people who feel led to for-profit ventures?"

"I know of another guy who used to be a high-flying executive for a pharmaceuticals firm but recently quit so that he could start a consulting firm in Japanese business space. He's not even Japanese, but of German and Canadian background. But he and his wife speak fluent Japanese, and not only do they seek to be a Christian witness in a heavily irreligious country, but they also seek to infuse the Japanese marketplace with Christian ethics. He's now trying to think through how to make it easier for those without jobs to start their own businesses in Japan. It's pretty incredible."

"This is great," he said with some exasperation. "But I feel called to be an engineer."

Bridge paused, raising an eyebrow. "We're not talking about Jared, eh?"

He caught himself and smiled. "I'm trying to figure things out too."

"If you still feel called to use what you've learned in engineering, what are ways that you can use your skills to advance God's kingdom? It will take some self-awareness and scrutiny. This will be really difficult to put into practice, especially given the state of our economy, but what if we started thinking beyond the paycheck? What if we asked if the work we do contributes to the good in the world? Or does it contribute evil?"

"That gets really complicated. I mean, Mobiship actually helps with the tracking of weapons."

"That, in itself, isn't bad. The question is: Does the tracking of weapons actually help make this a safer world or a more destructive one? I know that there's lots of dangerous room to wiggle here, but just be honest with it. At the end of your life, can you say without regret that you helped more than hurt? Would Jesus be proud of the way you now choose to spend your life? Don't worry about the past. Figure out what to do now. Can you say that your work from now on honors God in the best way you know? You'll have to keep asking others for input so you're not just rationalizing your paycheck. But do you hear what I'm saying?"

"Some people can't make that choice," he said, trying not to sound defensive. "I mean, they might not have the privilege to turn down a job because they need to put food on the table for their family."

"Sure," she said. "That will be true of many. But it's not true for you, eh?"

Ouch, he thought. That felt a little close to home.

"I'm not trying to make you feel guilty," she said, picking up on his wince. "I just want to help you find the freedom you're yearning for. Don't you want to work at a place where you believe in what you do? Wouldn't that make work so much more enjoyable? Or when you have to put in the hours, that the suffering will feel worth it?"

He nodded. It would be great to work at a place where he felt like he was doing more good than harm. It would be a nice feeling to wake up each morning at least knowing that what he was doing was worth it and that Jesus would be proud of him. That feeling seemed foreign.

"So, how can you see yourself being a world changer?" she asked.

"Ha, it looks like you're trying to get me to cross a line," he said.

"If the shoe fits . . ."

Stephen stared at the diagram in its entirety. Up to now, he would've said that he was already along the continuum in some way. He might be learning to hear God's voice better, but he would still consider himself a follower of Jesus. He also could learn how to give away power and authority in more effective ways, but he was still a leader in the church. But it's at this last piece that he felt foreign. He didn't feel like a world changer. He didn't have a sense of call or understand how his work was actually a vocation.

He didn't say much after that, lost in his own thoughts. Bridge's

following questions were answered with an unusual inatten-
tiveness. He managed to thank her for spending the time with
him and said he had much to think about. Then he got up, and
instead of walking straight back to the parking structure, he took
a left toward the Warren Mall.

PATH

Warren Mall was a grassy plot of land on campus, surrounded by science labs. On top of one of the buildings, a replica of a house was built at an angle, perched precariously on the corner as if it were going to fall. It felt as dizzying as his thoughts.

He was at the bottom of a hill, staring up a ten-foot-wide path that was covered with hexagonal tiles of multicolored slate, which made it look like the back of a rattlesnake. It was called the Snake Path. It wound up the hill toward Geisel Library, which in silhouette against the sunset looked even more like a giant hand reaching for fruit. In the seeming absence of guidance, he could understand the temptation to want to be like God. A giant brown version of Milton's *Paradise Lost* stood on his right, and behind him on one of the science labs words etched in neon flashed at irregular rhythms. They alternated between the Seven Deadly Sins and Seven Heavenly Virtues, as if blurred in a postmodern haze. It felt like the campus was sticking out its collective tongue at God.

As he started up the Snake Path, he traveled down a familiar road of thought.

Why did I choose to be an engineer?

The only thing giving him hope at work was Jared. But the tedious work, the late nights, the pressure. And for what? So that shipments can be tracked more easily? So that we can make money? There must be more to work than toil. Perhaps he should've gone into ministry instead? He walked slowly up the steep incline with his hands behind his back, feeling each step under his soles.

On one hand, his job gave him some perks: a love of technology, a steady income to provide for his family, an opportunity to care for his coworkers and be light in a dark place. These were all good things. But if he was honest with himself, the job was a security blanket.

Am I selling out?

Step.

But on the other hand, perhaps full-time ministry was a case of idealizing something on the other side of the fence. Honestly, he didn't know if he had the relational energy for full-time ministry. He loved solving technical problems—there was a certain thrill to figuring things out—and he had expertise and experience in this area. Was God in this? Wouldn't there be some sort of worship that could come from his work? But it would be hard to claim, if his ultimate aim was security.

Step.

Perhaps there was a another way—a way to serve God more fully yet still stay in the field. Perhaps there could be a sense of call outside of full-time ministry. *Shouldn't my work also be ministry? Aren't we all ministers?*

Step.

Work should be meaningful. If all things are reconciled, then work doesn't have to be toil, sweat on the brow. *What would the kingdom of God look like for me at work?* In Christ, it could be redeemed. He looked up again at the giant silhouette of forbidden fruit.

Step.

Perhaps there's another use for shipment tracking. Something that could be a blessing to others and the world.

Step.

Yet stay profitable, to bless employees and their families.

Step.

Encrypted so it couldn't be tracked. Passive so that it wouldn't bleed energy.

Step.

Accountability for nonprofits? Food. Supplies. Foreign aid. Accountability tools for government aid?

Step.

That actually could work. Donors and taxpayers would love to know that the aid their organizations or governments give is actually getting to the people who need it, at a fraction of the cost of assigning UN monitors.

Step. Step. Step.

He found himself on top of the hill, standing at the end of the path, which opened up into a wide concrete plaza. The path turned into a large mosaic of a snake's head. He was at Snakehead, a place where Bridge said students often prayed. In his own head, he heard the line: *And he will crush your head, and you will strike his heel.* Through Jesus, the enemy will be defeated.

Stephen, as one made in God's image, began to jump up and down and stomp on the head. He didn't stop and must've looked crazy to the few college students who saw him, but he didn't care.

The curse had already been broken.

EPILOGUE

Next Steps

DIVISION

For the next few weeks, Stephen agonized over the decisions he would have to make. He knew that he would leave his current role. That was certain. But he hadn't mapped out his next steps.

Should I start a new company? If I started my new company, how would I get the capital? He hadn't figured out the answers, but he also didn't feel like he could figure these out while being on the job. Work was too consuming. He knew that he would have to give notice soon.

Though he was working out his business plan, his heart fretted more over what would become of the Bible study. It had been a place where he consistently found God present, and it certainly made work more enjoyable and meaningful. But he worried about their future. *Who would lead them? Would they continue? Would it last without him?*

Instead of bearing the burden on his own, he decided to seek counsel from the Bible study. Empowerment, right? They surprised him, supporting his desire to work for something that he would feel in his bones would be honoring to God. If he left, they would bless him.

"But what about you?" he asked.

"Us?" asked Jared. "Of course we'll miss you. But did you forget that you've already taught each of us how to lead this study? We've each had a couple of shots at it. Darren's *actually* getting better."

"Punk," growled Darren. But he did have a big grin.

"The study will go on," said Sherrie. "Don't worry." Sherrie put her arm around Casey, who gave a knowing smile back at her, then at Stephen. He hadn't noticed it before, but he could be fooled into thinking they were related.

Then they prayed for him and tears fell down Stephen's face. He would miss all of this, all that God had done, all that he would do in each of them.

He gave his notice and expected to slip quietly out of the door. He'd seen it done many times before him. But the company surprised him: instead of someone from human resources showing him the door, a senior director wanted to see him personally. He was completely caught off guard when Mobiship counteroffered, not wanting to lose him. Stephen held his ground, letting the director know that he intended to start a new company. When the director realized that it wasn't about the money, he switched tracks and asked if Stephen would be open to making it a division at Mobiship instead of his own separate company. He would have access to the technology, improve on it and apply it in new fields. Floored, but not without his wits, Stephen asked for time to think about it.

Over the next couple of days, he checked his options. He didn't have the capital to get the company up and running right away, so this would be a faster way to get started. Sure, he'd lose on the possible upside, but he could move forward without much of a delay. So he eventually agreed, but only after he was given a few concessions.

RALLY

Stephen moved out of his old office, but didn't have to go far. The space for the new division was just a floor up in the same building. He had his own office and a new conference room, where the Bible study now met. One huge benefit was that he was still able to meet with them on a weekly basis.

The first concession he secured was the hiring of a separate salesperson who handled marketing and customer relations for the new division. Through the networks of the new hire, governmental and nongovernmental relief agencies became interested clients. With Mobiship Aid solutions, they could guarantee the shipments of relief supplies and show how they were being distributed throughout the world. It also showed them where they were failing. Though that brought on a new set of challenges to these organizations, at least they knew. And it added to their credibility: the nonprofits quickly realized that their donors felt a greater trust with the organization if they were to use Mobiship Aid technology, and so it increased giving. Even before the products went to market, many major nonprofits were already buzzing about it. A ministry was about to be born.

Getting the new products ready for market would come more quickly because of another Mobiship concession: Jared joined his team. One afternoon, Stephen and Jared were catching up a bit, eating their lunches back in the cafeteria. Jared was excited about Casey's spiritual growth: "She's so close, dude."

They talked about her some more, and afterward Jared brought up something that he hadn't in weeks.

"Did you know that I went to the rally?"

"Rally?" asked Stephen.

"The one at UCSD. That worship night between UCSD Campus Ministries and the Cross Cultural Center."

He nodded, recalling Bridge telling him about it at the café. He still felt uncomfortable bringing it up and allowed it to get lost in the whirlwind of starting a new division. Still, he admitted that he knew: "Yeah, Bridge saw you slip out."

"Ah," he said in a rare moment of embarrassment. "It was Bridge's idea for me to be there. But I felt weird. For the first time in my life, I was surrounded by Christians of so many ethnicities who gathered specifically for the racial healing of the campus. The Campus Ministries brought mostly Asian Americans and Caucasians, while the Cross Cultural Center also brought many African Americans and Latino Americans. I couldn't let go of the fact that every part of me was represented in that room, in some way. Not four parts separated out, but everyone together."

Stephen nodded in affirmation and prayed that he would be helpful in the conversation.

"I wasn't myself, dude. I was paralyzed. I didn't know how to act. Should I go over to the black community? Or the Asian? In some ways, they're all a part of me. In other ways, I don't fit in. So I just sat in the back and kept to myself."

"Wow," said Stephen. "You? Keeping to yourself?"

"Weird, right? But it was great how people from the front kept saying that we were one in Jesus that night. Together. For a purpose. Not ignoring our cultures, but embracing them. It was powerful. And then, we all started to worship. And I felt that same sense of presence that I did on Catalina. God was with me, dude. It's hard to explain. And he told me that I wasn't a mistake, that all the parts of me are actually *one* in him. He put it all together, and it made sense to him. Each of these parts is actually reconciled. I am whole. In Jesus."

As he spoke, he was barely keeping back his tears. Stephen was amazed: he was always so excitable. To see him with such tenderness took him aback.

"Right after that happened, I had to get out of there. I didn't know anyone there, but I needed to talk to someone."

"What did you do?"

"I called Tyson. Remember? My buddy from college. I just wanted to know if I was hearing things correctly."

"What did he say?"

"What he usually says," said Jared, as he rubbed his tattoo. "'Sounds like God.'"

Stephen's eyes went to Jared's hand. "Hey, I've been meaning to ask . . . you said that you got an equal sign for your tattoo, but you have three bars, not two."

"You're *sharp*," Jared said, letting his tone drip with sarcasm, though he still smiled wide.

"So what does the third bar mean?"

"After I became a Christian, I realized that justice wasn't enough. Even if justice was served, it didn't mean we were reconciled. It's still important, but I was part of a bigger plan. So I added a third bar to represent the Trinity: God, Jesus and the Holy Spirit. I still seek justice, but also forgiveness and reconciliation. But it all happens through him. Like that night, he is always with me."

They were both silent for a moment. Stephen was deeply encouraged, both by the way the campus ministry served Jared in a way he couldn't, and now by the way Jared had embraced his faith. But he remembered the cycle, and that if he heard something from God, then he'd have to *respond*. So he asked another question: "So you heard from God that night. How will you respond?"

"I think I'm doing it. Since I'm reconciled, I can help others—particularly of other ethnicities—reconcile with each other. What's happening in me should flow out, right? So I got involved in the planning of an immigration rally, and we're having our big event this weekend. We're pushing for another round of the Dream Act. That's my first step, and I'm meeting tons of new people. And Karis has been cool the whole time too. She'll be there this weekend. You wanna go?"

He shook his head. "I'm still working out what I think about that. I'll need to pick your brain sometime. *Soon,* I promise. But, for now, we have a little division to grow. But I'm glad you're getting connected."

The last statement was true, but he still had worries that Jared's newfound activism would distract him from getting the division up and running. Stephen couldn't afford a misstep at this stage, and he wanted Jared to be fully focused on getting the code up on time. On a deeper level, Stephen hadn't figured out where he stood on immigration, and Jared's talk made him a little nervous. Still, he was only doing what he encouraged him to do: to be an agent of healing in the world around him. Maybe Jared would help him figure out where he should stand on the issue, and how it might relate to faith.

"You got it," Jared said. "Let me know when you want to talk about it."

Stephen glanced at the clock on the wall and realized that the lunch hour was almost over. "We should get back," he said. "Are you going to be able to get that code up by the deadline?"

"No problem, dude."

Stephen still looked worried.

"Boss," he said, "have I ever let you down?" And Jared gave him a strong jab in the shoulder. As Stephen rubbed his arm, he wondered if it would be okay to ask God to stop Jared from doing that anymore.

FOUR

Stephen had invited Bridge over to his place to have dinner with the family, and after the kids were sent to bed, they were enjoying cups of tea around his dining table.

At an opportune moment Stephen said, "I think we need to finish something."

"Right," Bridge winked.

Misun saw another conversation coming, so she excused herself. Bridge pulled out her folio one more time. She drew another arrow and the words *make disciples.*

"Here's the last part, and the most obvious: disciples make disciples. Discipleship and disciplemaking go hand in hand. In fact, if we don't have this in mind, we'll be shortsighted in the way we make disciples."

Stephen nodded but wanted to hear more.

"We have to keep 2 Timothy 2:2 in mind. Paul wrote to his protégé, Timothy, and he charged him with something absolutely profound. Let me look it up." She reached into her bag and pulled out her smartphone, and found the Scripture verse she was looking for: "'And the things you have heard me say in the presence of many witnesses entrust to reliable people who will also be qualified to teach others.'"

"Okay, help me figure that out."

"The verse walks through four generations of disciples. 'Heard me say' is Paul—*one*. He wrote to Timothy—*two*. Timothy should 'entrust to reliable people'—*three*. 'Who will also be qualified to teach others'—*four*. It goes down for *four* generations, and that's important. If you think only one generation, then obviously you don't have to pass it on at all."

"I got that one," he smirked. He couldn't help it.

She kept rolling, "If you think two, then you only have to pass it to someone else, like you to Jared. That's what most people think of discipleship."

Stephen was starting to get it. He jumped in. "But if I were thinking three generations, then I would invest in Jared so that he could invest in others."

"Right, but can you see the problem there?"

"Ah," he said slowly. "Jared wouldn't learn how to disciple someone who could disciple someone. It would stop."

"Exactly," she beamed. "A four-generational mindset is needed for continued multiplication. You have to think about how to develop disciples who know how to develop disciples who develop disciples. And that's really different than just investing in someone—*two*—or even investing in someone to invest in someone—*three*. They need to keep on thinking how the investment will continue."

"This is better than a management book, and it's right here in the Bible," said Stephen. "Maybe that's why no business has lasted for more than two thousand years."

She smiled: "So this model continues to replicate. World changers reach out to skeptics, and this continues again and again, in the context of community. Got it?"

He nodded as she ripped the page off the folio and handed it to him.

"I will guard this with my life," he joked as he pulled the diagram up to his chest.

"Live it out instead," she said with a smile. "So, ready to give that talk?" She had invited him to speak at her campus ministry on the topic of vocation.

"I haven't been more nervous about anything in a while, including starting up the new company. I don't want to be boring."

"Don't worry. Just tell your story."

PULLING BACK
THE CURTAINS

THE NEED FOR THE
REAL LIFE CONTINUUM

As a kid, I loved jigsaw puzzles. My process wasn't particularly unique: I'd look for the corners first. They were easy to pick out. Then I'd seek out the edges. After I had a completed frame, I'd find a distinctive element in the picture, preferably close to the edge, and start searching for those pieces. It was absolutely satisfying when one of these elements would connect with another one or to the edge. Then I'd fill in the rest. Of course, the more pieces there were, the harder the puzzle was to complete. But if I had the box top with the completed picture, it would just be a matter of time. Without it, the puzzle would be impossible to finish.

Discipleship can feel like a five-thousand-piece jigsaw puzzle without a box top. We have lots of pieces to cover if we want to help someone be like Jesus if he were on earth today: spiritual formation, community, evangelism, leadership development, vocation, finances, family, justice, serving the poor and the mission, just to name a few. Someone might have described what the puzzle is supposed to look like—like a shimmering lake on a forest's edge or a hobbit's home on a rolling grassy slope—but without a concrete image, those phrases are of little help when you're choosing between the blue or green pieces. Without the box top, another temptation kicks in: to ignore the completed picture and treat each piece separately. But that's not the point of the puzzle: it's supposed to come together in some way.

The Real Life Continuum is an offering of what a box top for discipleship might look like. It's an attempt to make sense out of the various pieces of discipleship, pulling it together in some simple and coherent form without losing some oft-neglected pieces. At the same time, it's designed to be of practical use to any disciplemaker today.

I had already been on staff with InterVarsity Christian Fellowship for seven years before I saw what would eventually become the Real Life Continuum. My wife accepted an invitation to graduate school in San Diego, which actually broke our hearts at the time. Boston had been my home for eleven years, and the thought of uprooting out of a spiritually rich community into a place where we knew only one other person felt like a poor tradeoff. But after arriving, the sun and surf made it easier. And we clung tightly to that one dear friend.

In the move, I stayed with InterVarsity and met my new boss's boss, Chris Nichols, who oversaw the work in San Diego County. During this season, he'd become a mentor to me, and he introduced me to one of his creations: a diagram with an arrow and five stages across the top marked *skeptic, seeker, follower, leader* and *world changer*. It was simple and unadorned, but it pulled together the many threads I had seen in Scripture into one tapestry.

It accomplished two things immediately. Back then, evangelism and discipleship were sworn enemies. If you pursued evangelism, then the ministry was doomed to be shallow, unable to plumb the depths of theology and spirituality. But if you pursued discipleship, then the ministry was thought to become irrelevant to the vast majority of the campus who had yet to believe. But this diagram demolished the either-or arguments and reconciled these two ministry paths as part of the same journey.

The second thing it did was to redirect the aim of our ministry. We weren't just empowering student leaders and potential staff for *our* ministry. We weren't just getting them ready to pad church attendance statistics when they graduated. It reminded us that we were investing in influencers who, we hoped, would not merely change the church, but would also change the world. Spiritual formation, ministry and social activism were no longer at odds, competing for the same resources, but could play together in the same sandbox.

Two years after that meeting, Chris left to take a new role, directing the work in New England. In the vacancy, I took over his role for the next five years. During that time, I wrote a doctoral dissertation to synthesize what I'd been learning through classes, research and campus ministry. Up to that time, I had been seminary trained by Boomers, but I'd spent half of my vocational life ministering to Xers and the other half ministering to Millennials. Though both were postmodern generations, they felt very different. But in a time when the talk about postmodern and emerging ministries was the rage, I felt that the Millennials were being overlooked. Each generation has its own flavor, its own needs, its own way of seeing and doing things, and its own questions about faith. If we let one generation monopolize what discipleship should look like for all the other generations, without understanding where each generation is coming from, then we may fail to entice and inspire rising generations to become mature disciples in Christ. On the flipside, knowing more about how each generation operates and sees the world could empower us to help them explore what faith might look like and live it out—a faith that is fully biblical and yet fully their own.

On top of it all, I believed that the perspective of each generation could help us address blind spots and find commonalities to create a more robust model of discipleship usable for everyone—one that could be flexible enough to be nuanced for each generation alive today. After all, regardless of our generation, the destination is the same: we're all trying to be like Jesus if he lived in our culture and time to do what he did for the reasons he did them."

To make the model more practical, I described the goal of disciplemaking for each stage:

skeptic	build trust
seeker	challenge toward next steps
follower	train to recognize God's voice and obey it
leader	give power and authority
world changer	cast vision for broader impact

The additions didn't merely give us clarity about our discipleship process, but they also gave us marching orders. The community aspect was also made more explicit, to encourage a more communal model of discipleship. Through this diagram, we had a stronger sense of what to do with students *at each stage,* wherever they may happen to fall on this continuum. On the Real Life Continuum, these phrases were shorted to five words: *trust, challenge, recognize, empower* and *envision.*

The latest and final additions to the diagram occurred more recently. InterVarsity has recently placed discipleship—alongside growth, evangelism and leadership development—as a major area of focus for our national movement in the next five years. The task force for the discipleship initiative came up with a simple yet brilliant process to describe what staff were already doing intuitively as disciplemakers: *hear* God's Word, *respond* and then *debrief* the experience. This cycle could be used at any stage of the Real Life Continuum, and it made more explicit the inter-action between the disciplemaker, the disciple and God's Spirit. I couldn't leave it out.

In all, the Real Life Continuum not only helps clarify the disci-plemaking process; it can be useful in tracking your own devel-opment as a disciple as well. I hope that this diagram will assist in empowering the next generation of Christian leaders who are full of vision for God's kingdom, love in Jesus' name and intimacy and power through the Holy Spirit.

WALKTHROUGH PART 1

Skeptic to World Changer

It does feel ironic to offer a discipleship *diagram:* many post-moderns may be turned off by such an approach. It could feel too canned. Still, this model is useful as a simple mnemonic aid to remember the purpose and process of becoming a disciple.

To be clear, these stages are not meant to be a hard-wired, sequential path. Some people won't go in order. They might fall back into skepticism after following Jesus for a long time. Others may already seek to be world changers and yet still be learning the basics of following Jesus. Someone might be in two stages at once: a leader in the ministry yet relearning how to hear God's voice in a new season of life. Nevertheless, identifying these subplots in the story of leadership development can be helpful so that we can know what future kingdom leaders may need as they mature in faith and ministry.

SKEPTIC: BUILD TRUST

A *skeptic* doesn't trust a Christian or Christians as a whole. With skeptics, trust must be built or rebuilt. In the past, offering a Christian faith that was both intellectually robust and rationally sound often built credibility for skeptics. But today, rational apologetics can actually break trust, especially if it's used to start an argument or to make someone feel belittled. Highlighting absolute truth, without anything else, reinforces the stereotype that Christians are intolerant of others in our postmodern culture.

In creating trust today, two areas need to be highlighted. First, *relational* trust is crucial. In *I Once was Lost* by Don Everts and Doug Schaupp, they offer five do's and don'ts in building trust. *Don't* get defensive, feel bruised, avoid, judge or argue. *Do* pray, learn, bond, affirm and welcome. These are ways to help build trust on a personal, relational level. (Read their book for more tips.)

Building *communal* trust is also helpful, so that someone doesn't just trust a Christian, but begins to trust Christians or Christianity as a whole. Here, it is important not merely to be nice, but also to offer a humble voice showing how Christianity is actually *good* for the wider world.

- In what ways can you build trust with an unbeliever? What steps will you take in the next week to build (or rebuild) trust?

- In what ways in the following week can you share the Christian story or highlight Christian activities that will not only build trust with a person, but also build trust with the Christian community as a whole?

SEEKER: CHALLENGE TOWARD NEXT STEPS

Many Christians don't differentiate between skeptics and seekers. Grace-heavy Christians continue to make deposits in the trust accounts of unbelievers without thoughtfully challenging them to next steps in their spiritual journey. Truth-heavy Christians challenge unbelievers about their wrongdoings without any foundation of trust and are thus unheard. Knowing the difference between a skeptic and a seeker is crucial in helping both mature in faith.

A seeker is different from a skeptic in one very important way: *trust*. Where skeptics don't trust Christians or Christ, a seeker has had some positive interactions with the Christian community and trusts them to an extent. Though seekers are not yet ready to give their lives to Jesus' leadership, they enjoy being in the community and are investigating the faith's relevance to their lives.

Because they have some measure of trust, seekers are more receptive to input. A thoughtful challenge to pursue something deeper with Jesus is often taken as a sign of care and honesty instead of coercion. Since the seeker already has some level of trust with the Christian community, humbly invite them to take another step in their journey with Jesus.

Any step is fine, whether it's an invitation to a Bible study, a chance to serve in a service project, or a commitment to investigate Jesus more deeply. Whatever you do, offer chances to grow and serve. Christians need to overcome their fears in asking their seeking friends to take more steps, particularly service projects, because transformation often occurs when seekers take steps of faith, no matter how small.

At some point, seekers can be challenged to give their lives to Jesus—to let him be the leader and rescuer of their lives. The Big

Story, which I describe in my previous book, *The Story,* could be helpful here. If they do make a decision to follow Jesus, help that person express that new allegiance in front of the community, such as in a baptism or through a testimony. A challenge to share their story with the wider community will help new believers identify with the larger community of faith.

- This week, in what next step will you challenge an unbeliever to move toward Jesus?

- Identify someone who might be ready to hear the Big Story from you this week. What next steps will you need to take in preparing to share that story? How will you invite that person to follow Jesus?

FOLLOWER: TRAIN TO RECOGNIZE GOD'S VOICE AND OBEY

A *follower* is someone who has pledged allegiance to Jesus and his kingdom. If a seeker becomes a follower, disciplemakers still need to know how to help them take their next steps. This is where evangelism and discipleship come together as one process.

The main aim of a follower is to learn how to recognize God's voice and obey it. That's it. All of the spiritual rhythms are geared toward this end. We read our Bibles and memorize biblical passages because the more we know how God has spoken to people in the past, it will help us recognize him more in our present day. The more we pray, the more we are open to his prompting since we've given God more space in our lives. The more we connect in Christian community, the more we are able to discern his voice. These kinds of spiritual disciplines are not an end in and of themselves—which leads to legalism—but are wonderful *means* to hearing and recognizing God's voice. So that when he speaks, we can reply like Samuel and say, "Speak, for your servant is listening" (1 Samuel 3:10). It seems that early Christians had the expectation that the Spirit of God would communicate with them and that his guidance would be real and palpable (John 16:13-15). We nurture our souls through recognizing his voice in the everyday.

This, however, needs to be made clear: the way God's voice is communicated to each person can be quite unique. For one person, God's voice could come through the Bible itself as a felt prompting as she reads. For another, it could come through the voice of a trusted friend or a sermon heard on Sunday. It could also come as an impression or a vision that a Christian sees in his mind's eye. Perhaps being overcome by nature's beauty or reflecting on a lyric in a song speaks to another of God's voice. God speaks through it all, and it would be a shame to try to limit God in the way he speaks to his followers. But that doesn't mean it's a free-for-all. Everything should be checked through the Scriptures and the community of believers: "Prophets should speak, and the others should weigh carefully what is said" (1 Corinthians 14:29).

But hearing is not enough. Jesus himself said that the difference between people who build their houses on solid bedrock or shifting sands is not in the quality of teaching they hear, but in their obedience to what they've heard (Matthew 7:24-27). It's in obeying that the change comes. The question that a disciple maker must keep asking is, "What is God saying to you, and what are you going to do about it?"

- In what ways can you help someone this week learn more about how to hear God's voice in everyday life and obey it?

- How do other spiritual disciplines fit into hearing God's voice, and how does that inform your next steps this week?

LEADER: GIVE POWER AND AUTHORITY

Leadership development and discipleship are often considered different fields, but they come together in this model. Discipleship, however, is more than just growing close to God in a pietistic sense. When someone has become more comfortable in the practice of hearing God's voice—particularly in community—then they can follow God's leadership into the influence of others. What we have, we give away.

So we help others become *leaders:* a leader is someone who is influencing others. It doesn't need to be a formal role, as in a church or a Christian organization, or it can be informal through relationships. A disciple doesn't merely receive from Christian community, but is also called to serve and contribute (1 Corinthians 12:7). To empower this service, a disciplemaker finds ways to offer power and authority (Luke 9:1).

Power is any resource leaders need to help them influence others. It may mean helping secure funding and other physical resources needed to fulfill their leadership duties. It could be praying for the power of the Holy Spirit to be present in the leaders' lives. Finding resources for the other leaders also empowers them. They'll sense the disciplemaker's confidence in them because she is willing to sacrifice time and energy so they can have the resources they need to lead.

In addition to power, a disciplemaker should also work toward giving leaders authority. It's basically decision-making responsibility. They offer public words of encouragement for the leaders under their care, showing their confidence in them. He also creates ministry opportunities so that they have a particular realm to lead in. The disciplemaker seeks to make increasingly fewer on-the-field decisions, so that new leaders can make their own decisions. Of course, disciplemakers still offer feedback for leaders' development, but they take great care not to undermine their leadership. Ultimately, Jesus gives his power and authority to all believers—to bless and serve others.

- In what ways can you bestow more power on someone who is growing in leadership? What resources can you offer them this week?

- In what ways can you bestow greater authority on a leader? What next steps would you take this week in this area?

WORLD CHANGER: GIVE VISION FOR BROADER IMPACT

Jesus once told his disciples: "Very truly I tell you, whoever believes in me will do the works I have been doing, and they will do even greater things than these" (John 14:12). It's mind-boggling that Jesus thought that our impact could be greater than his own.

So we help disciples become world changers. Serving the Christian community isn't the end. It's just training. What matters most is our ability and willingness to serve people beyond the walls of the church, whether in our workplaces, communities or places with people we haven't yet met. *World changers* seek to bless the world around them. "World" here doesn't mean the entire planet or even everyone in it. That's impossible: that's God's job. But we are called to bless and influence the "worlds" we've been given, however small they may be.

For disciplemakers, we develop *world changers* by helping them envision their calling for this season. To help, it's good to discern their gifts and passions, for they can give clues to what a particular calling might be. But we ultimately help them see how they might be a part of changing the world and ask God to give them conviction about their next steps. With any need or location, keep asking: "What would the kingdom of God look like if it showed up here?" The kingdom is needed in every area of society and life, but helping rising leaders envision a concrete way to advance this kingdom is a great gift a leader can give to her followers.

- What gifts and passions does the person you disciple display? In what ways can you help them explore these areas more this week?

- In what ways can you help envision a calling or vocation with a rising leader this week?

WALKTHROUGH
PART 2

Community, Disciplemaking
and the Holy Spirit

Other contexts and processes fill out the rest of the Real Life Continuum.

COMMUNITY OF THE BIG STORY

In disciplemaking, some of us cherish one-on-one meetings. It's the easiest place to go deep, be intimate. But is it the best way to disciple someone? It may very well be done as a necessity: coordinating multiple calendars is often frustrating, providing evidence of the Fall! Even if we get everyone in one room, getting them to like and trust each other can become yet another exercise in futility. Yet the God-in-flesh thought it necessary to make disciples in a community of twelve. He invested time and energy into *them,* and sure, he had individual conversations, but he spent most of his time with his oft-cantankerous students as a group. It makes me ask: Is it even possible to disciple people *well* if we're only meeting one-on-one?

Although it's tempting to make the disciplemaking process individualistic, it's important to do this in community. Discipling in community has a way of deeply reinforcing what has been taught, as people in the group encourage and challenge each other instead of merely relying on the leader.

- What next steps can you take this week to develop disciplemaking communities?

- Who else would you need to invite to the meeting to make this work?

MAKE DISCIPLES

I've rarely heard spiritual formation and disciplemaking in the same breath, as if disciplemaking didn't inform our discipleship. Have we unintentionally divorced the two? Jesus said quite clearly that we should "make disciples of all nations" (Matthew 28:19). So, are we actually mature disciples if we're not *making* disciples? Put more bluntly, isn't every Christian called to be both a *disciple* and a *disciplemaker?*

Therefore, disciples disciple others—whether they are skeptics, seekers, followers, leaders or world changers. The disciplemaking *process* that follows happens at each stage through a three-part cycle, based on Luke 10:

Hear. In verses 2-16, the seventy-two disciples listen to Jesus' instructions. They take time to hear what he has to say. Today, we also need to create spaces for God speak to the community. Yes, God will speak through the personal reading of Scripture, preaching and Bible studies. At the same time, creating spaces for God to speak through prayer, silence or divine promptings also helps highlight what God might be saying. Be open to the many ways God may choose to speak and use discernment to encourage or correct words that are shared in the group, keeping these four things in mind: Is it biblical? What does the community think? What is the fruit of that word? Does it create fear?

Respond. The seventy-two then go out according to Jesus' instructions to heal the sick and cast out demons. They respond by going out two-by-two. In verse 17, it's implied that they do what he asked.

In this way, any Scripture study, any prayer meeting, anything that you do together as a community needs to point to a specific application point. It's about responding to God's Word, since Jesus said that the only difference between someone who builds his house on the rock and on the sand is not in the quality of teaching they receive, but in their response—whether they choose to obey what they hear or to ignore it.

Debrief. In verses 17-24, Jesus' disciples return in triumph. In debriefing them, Jesus offers two things: encouragement and correction. Disciples will regularly need to hear your encouragement and correction to know if they're on the right track. And a disciplemaker can offer wisdom to help disciples interpret their experiences correctly, so that they continue to build their faith lives on the right perspectives.

- This week, identify someone that God is calling you to disciple. What next steps will you take to invite that person to a disciple-making community?

- In what ways can you create spaces for people to hear God's voice this week? How will you help them discern what they are hearing?

- In what ways can you help someone this week respond to God's Word, whether in Scripture or in life?

- What experience can you help someone interpret in the following week? What can you affirm? What would you correct?

HOLY SPIRIT

Of course, all of this work—the hearing of God's voice, responding in action to what was heard and debriefing the experience—is done by the guidance, leading and discernment of the Holy Spirit. We respond only through the power of his Spirit. And we debrief in the presence of his Spirit, to make sure that we're learning the right things. The Spirit lives in us, teaching us everything, and reminds us of all that Jesus taught (John 14:17, 26). He is, after all, the Counselor.

My fear is that too many Christians act as if we can work without the Holy Spirit. I had heard someone say once that the American Trinity is God, Jesus and the Bible. We often take out the Spirit. Without denigrating the need for and the authority of the Holy Scriptures, we need the Holy Spirit to empower the work he has called us to (Acts 1:8).

- In what ways does the Holy Spirit influence your disciplemaking?

- What steps would you take to create more space for the Holy Spirit in our disciplemaking processes?

THE REAL LIFE CONTINUUM
IN REAL LIFE

When we introduced the Real Life Continuum in our ministry, it integrated our mission and gave us a clearer direction about what we were trying to accomplish. Motivation and inspiration flowed into our work, as we were excited about developing world changers—people who would not only bless the church but also the wider world beyond its walls. It also reconciled competing interests in evangelism and discipleship and helped us see how they were a part of one stream.

Not only did it change our vision of ministry, but it also changed the way we did it. If we truly believed that all followers of Jesus were to recognize God's voice in the everyday and obey what they heard, it would need to find expression in every level of our ministry. When our senior leadership made major decisions, we created times to listen to God's voice in the middle of our deliberations. When we gathered all of the thirty or so staff in the division together, not only did we study Scripture, but we also waited in silence. Our student leadership teams and prayer meetings were also affected, as we taught our students to recognize the ways God may speak to us. In campus gatherings, we'd often invite people to hear God's voice in response to a sermon or a worship set. Prayer wasn't meant to be a monologue, but a dialogue.

This has also spilled over into the way I speak in other settings. I remember vividly when I was invited to guest speak at my church in San Diego. I delivered what I thought was a good sermon.

When I asked for feedback from the senior pastor, he did a thorough job. But it was one question in the middle of his evaluation that drew me up short. He asked, "What do you do when God speaks to you at the end of your sermon?" I stared at him blankly, not even having a category for what he had just said.

So now, at the end of a talk, I don't just pray and step down. Instead, I wait and listen to hear if God might want to direct the response time after the sermon. Often, that time is more memorable than what I had just preached—and I hope I'm not *that* bad a teacher! At more recent speaking events, I've invited unbelievers to hear what God might be saying to them directly, and they often actually hear God speaking to them. In response to hearing God's voice, they've committed their lives to Jesus. One word from God is worth a thousand sermons.

In another example, I've recently had the chance to teach this material at an InterVarsity statewide conference in Virginia. Four hundred and eighty college students crammed into a youth camp an hour away from Roanoke. The organizers of this conference actually wove the Real Life Continuum into every aspect of the camp. Testimonies were offered by those who had made transitions along the Continuum: a skeptic who had already suffered through three heart surgeries told of how he became a seeker after befriending InterVarsity students, a seeker became a follower through the witness of a Christian community, a follower who needed a vision of faith that went beyond meeting his own needs stepped up to be a small group leader, and an alumnus who used to be a large group coordinator transformed into a world changer—she works with an organization to eradicate human trafficking and contemporary slavery. Even the book table was organized along the Continuum.

When I taught the Continuum throughout the weekend, it was great to cast a large vision of the Christian life, one that was meant to change, in the very least, the world around them. In the evening, I shared that being a follower of Jesus meant listening to his voice and described how that might work. One Christian described how he knew about God and a great deal of theology but, up until that night, had no real experience with God. When asked what he heard that night, he heard that he was God's child—which gave him an experience of God that would encourage him to continue thriving in his faith.

Since we had been working through the Real Life Continuum throughout the weekend, I could tailor a response specifically for each stage. When I challenged seekers to give their lives to Jesus, the student who gave the skeptic-to-seeker testimony became a follower. With this framework, he can also look ahead to being a leader in the fellowship and then a world changer beyond the fellowship. When he made a commitment to follow Jesus that night, he knew at a basic level that the path of faith included spiritual formation, leadership development and the mission. And the community around him, through the Holy Spirit, would now have a clearer picture of how to disciple him along the way.

So, as Jesus charged: "Therefore go and make disciples of all nations, baptizing them in the name of the Father and of the Son and of the Holy Spirit, and teaching them to obey everything I have commanded you. And surely I am with you always, to the very end of the age."

ACKNOWLEDGMENTS

Like a good Asian kid, my first thanks goes out to Mom and Dad for this book. After living with them for eighteen years and then loving them for two decades more, it's almost crazy that I can say with complete honesty that I have never questioned their love for Jesus, and their faith has profoundly affected mine.

Since this is a discipleship book, I also *wanted* to thank everyone who had ever invested in me. But knowing that it would be a futile process to do so, given the space constraints and my complete inability to juggle more than a few details, I didn't try. Instead, I'll thank those who directly contributed to the publishing of this book. First, the following readers gave me early and helpful feedback in their "spare" time: Phil Bowling-Dyer, Doug Creviston, Janell Gibson, Joe Ho, Jason Jensen, Kathy Khang, Janna Louie, Isaac Pollock, Jamie Wilson and Dora Yiu. Thank you.

Without Coast Vineyard—my home church of seven years—and the wider Association of Vineyard Churches, I wouldn't have learned much about hearing God's voice. Much of the material on hearing God's voice comes from experiences in their communities, who stretch me in the ways of his Spirit without acting *too* freaky. I'm also grateful for the opportunity to work with the Discipleship Working Group at Lausanne's Younger Leaders Gathering 2012. They've affirmed and solidified my thinking, and I've borrowed heavily from the pithy words of our facilitator, Elizabeth Paul. She knows what she's talking about.

And when I write, I basically loot the caves of InterVarsity Christian Fellowship and bring the treasure back out for the wider church world to see. Andy Crouch deserves mention, since his ideas are sprinkled throughout the book. I borrowed even more heavily from Doug Schaupp and Don Everts, especially for the first half of this book. Jason Jensen and Jon Ball created the *hear-respond-debrief* cycle outright, and it's used here with their permission. And the lion's share of the thanks goes to Chris Nichols, who first created the five-stage skeleton of the Real Life Continuum. He not only let me use it but allowed me to add to it as well. It takes a big heart to let someone run with your idea and then publish it with modifications.

The team at InterVarsity Press is a delight. In particular, Al Hsu has a knack of pulling my head out of the mud and getting me back on track. And I'm thankful to the rest of the crew that does the heavy lifting, catching my mistakes and getting this message out to readers in a more beautiful and compelling way.

Of course, my wife, Jinhee, deserves much of the credit as well. Without her love, support and her generous hand with our two young boys, this book would merely be electrons in the grey-and-white matter that resides between my ears. Things don't last long there.

Finally, it might be considered cliché to thank Jesus. It's just as expected from a Christian author as it is from an R&B singer. But I find it's still good for my soul to acknowledge that apart from him, I can do nothing.

NOTES

Before We Start

page 10   "remaining in him is absolutely critical": In the first ten verses of John 15, Jesus repeats the word *remain* eleven times.

page 11   "long obedience in the same direction": From the title of a classic Eugene Peterson book, *A Long Obedience in the Same Direction* (Downers Grove, IL: InterVarsity Press, 1980).

page 11   "Love God, love others": Matthew 22:37-40.

page 12   "sent together to heal": James Choung, *True Story: A Christianity Worth Believing In* (Downers Grove, IL: InterVarsity Press, 2008), p. 215.

page 13   helping our friends: That's how Elizabeth Paul, director of communications for 3DM, defined discipleship at Lausanne's North American Younger Leaders Gathering in Madison, Wisconsin, on July 25, 2012.

page 13   Brian McLann, "Emerging Values," *Leadership,* Summer 2003, p. 39.

page 13   "being salt and light": Matthew 5:13-16.

Prologue: Generations

page 33   "stuff in red letters": Some printed Bibles have Jesus' words printed in red.

page 33   "construction worker by trade": The word translated *carpenter* is a more general term like *builder, craftsman* or even *engineer.* Most of the time in Greek literature, it is translated *stonemason.*

page 38   "Men resemble the times": Jean Twenge, *Generation Me* (New York: Free Press, 2006), p. 3.

page 40   "our spiritual question was 'What is true?'": I first heard about generational spiritual questions from Andy Crouch, author of *Culture Making* (Downers Grove, IL: InterVarsity Press, 2008), while we were on InterVarsity staff together in the Boston area. He had offered the spiritual question for Boomers and Xers.

page 42   worldview shifts, five hundred years: Brian McLaren, *A New Kind of Christian* (San Francisco: Jossey-Bass, 2001), p. 15.

page 42   Pilate, "What is truth?": John 18:38.

page 43   "most aborted generation in history": William Strauss and
               Neil Howe, *Generations* (New York: William Morrow,
               1991), p. 324.

page 44   the name Generation X: John M. Ulrich, "Introduction: Gen-
               eration X, A (Sub)Cultural Genealogy," in *GenXegesis: Essays
               on Alternative Youth (Sub)Cultures*, ed. John M. Ulrich and
               Andrea L. Harris (Madison, WI: Popular Press, 2003), p. 3.

page 47   "Others call them Mosaics": George Barna, "The Church
               and the Mosaic Generation," www.homileticsonline.com/
               subscriber/interviews/barna.asp.

page 47   "*emerging* or *postmodern* generations": In May 2007,
               Ryan Bolger, who conducted a five-year survey that
               became the book *Emerging Churches* (Grand Rapids: Baker
               Academic, 2005), found that the Emergent Village and
               leaders in emerging churches weren't making distinctions
               between the two generations. Neither does Jean Twenge,
               author of *Generation Me* (New York: Free Press, 2006),
               which includes everyone born in the 1970s, '80s and '90s.

page 49   "Millenials can heed moral exemplars": Neil Howe and
               William Strauss, *Millennials Rising* (New York: Vintage
               Books, 2000), p. 365.

page 50   "Millennials will definitely not want to be known as
               Gen Y": Jay Taubman, quoted in ibid., p. 7.

page 51   "a day-by-day plan to get there": For more on helping
               Millennials to create a plan, check out Meg Jay, *The De-
               fining Decade: Why Your Twenties Matter—And How to
               Make the Most of Them Now* (New York: Twelve, 2012).

page 52   "video games hijack religious language": For example,
               in the bestselling video game *Halo,* the enemy is the
               Covenant—known for its religion, conformity and lack
               of original thought.

page 53   "*Internet Generation, the New Silents,* or *Generation
               Z*": Scot McKnight used *iGen* to describe Millennials in
               "The Gospel for iGens," *Leadership Journal* 30 (Summer
               2009): 20-24. Jean Twenge also used *iGeneration* for
               both Generation X and Millennials. But Wikipedia.com,
               at the time of this writing, equates iGen with the gen-
               eration that comes after the Millennials.

pages 53-54 America's four-generation cycle: For more detail on gen-
               erational theory, read William Strauss and Neil Howe,

Generations (New York: William Morrow, 1991). To see some critiques, see rationalwiki.org/wiki/William_Strauss _and_Neil_Howe.

page 54   "society is equitable for all and no one gets left behind": Ibid., p. 366.

page 54   "the Silent Generation of 1925-1945": Ibid., p. 285.

page 54   "What is beautiful?": Coincidentally, the four spiritual questions of the day are mirrored in Greek philosophy, particularly in Plato's Universals: the Good, the Real, the True and the Beautiful. For Plato, the reality we experience is mere shadows cast by these higher ideals. They're also interrelated—what is the Good is also the Real, and the True is also the Beautiful—and all hint toward one overarching Universal, dubbed "the One" or "the Absolute." See www.warren-wilson.edu/~dmycoff/plato.html.

page 55   A 2002 Stanford study: B. J. Fogg, C. Soohoo and D. R. Danielson, "How Do Users Evaluate the Credibility of Websites?" (2000), www.consumer webwatch.org/pdfs/StanfordPTL.pdf.

Part 1: Skeptic

page 61   Jewish boys' memorization of the Torah: Rob Bell, *Velvet Elvis* (Grand Rapids: Zondervan, 2005), p. 126.

page 62   Galilean scholars versus their Judean counterparts: David Bivin, *New Light on the Difficult Words of Jesus* (Holland, MI: En-Gedi Resource Center, 2005), p. 3.

page 62   "Can anything good come from there?": John 1:46. Nazareth is in Galilee.

page 62   "cover yourself in the dust of their feet": Rabbi Yose ben Yoezer, *Mishnah*, Avot 1:4.

page 62   Peter walking on water: Matthew 14:22-33.

page 63   "fishing with their fathers, learning the trade": Matthew 4:18-22.

page 63   Jesus "had faith in us": Bell, *Velvet Elvis,* p. 134.

page 64   "skepticism against the Christian faith": The Barna Group, "Atheists and Agnostics Take Aim at Christians," June 11, 2007, www.barna.org/barna-update/article/ 12-faithspirituality/102-atheists-and-agnostics-take-aim-at-christians.

page 64   radical Christianity as threatening as radical Islam: Ibid.

page 65	"has to happen in relational trust": To learn more ways to build relational trust, read a great book on postmodern evangelism called *I Once Was Lost* (Downers Grove, IL: InterVarsity Press, 2008) by Don Everts and Doug Schaupp.
page 66	"Thomas, the disciple that was the most skeptical": John 20:24-28.
page 70	"Jesus can give us living water": "Thirst," an actual talk given by Doug Schaupp, coauthor of *I Once Was Lost,* August 25, 2011, University of Southern California, InterVarsity Trojan Christian Fellowship.
page 70	"That red cup messed with me": The Red Cup campaign was an actual outreach used by InterVarsity Christian Fellowship on many campuses: www.intervarsity.org/news/red-cups-new-role-campus.
page 70	the lady who wanted living water: John 4:1-42.
page 72	"awareness about sex trafficking": InterVarsity has done a major campus-wide justice invitational around this theme at Ohio State called "Price of Life," which brought together academics, politicians and nonprofit leaders to raise awareness and seek solutions around the slave trade: osupriceoflife.org.

Part 2: Seeker

page 76	"tree of the knowledge of good and evil": One of the architects of the Geisel Library, James Manning, "recalls that he held up his hand with fingers spread in a gesture to suggest the supporting structure that was finally accepted. Indeed, one of the symbolic overtones of the final design is of books held high above the earthbound." "Geisel Library: Urban Legends," compiled by Barbara Henderson and Charles (Bud) Stem, libraries.ucsd.edu/about/see-also/geisel-library-urban-legends.html.
page 80	"Actions are not self-interpretive": An early mentor of mine, Rich Lamb, would say this all the time. I don't know where he got it.
page 87	"this stage . . . deciding to become a Christian": Doug Schaupp said this while teaching on his book *I Once Was Lost,* which had surveyed thousands of college students about how they became Christians.
page 90	"give a reason for the hope that you have": 1 Peter 3:15.

page 90	"the Big Story": My previous book, *True Story: A Christianity Worth Believing In* (Downers Grove, IL: InterVarsity Press, 2008), presents a new way to share the old gospel today.
page 98	"No verse or chapter numbers. Just the Bible": Manuscript study is the signature way we study the Bible in Inter-Varsity. Use the link for resources and more information: www.intervarsity.org/Bible-studies. Also see Lindsay Olesberg, *The Bible Study Handbook* (Downers Grove, IL: InterVarsity Press, 2012).
page 99	"it was clear that he thought he was God": Mark 8:27-38, but it's also hinted at in Mark 4:41 and 6:50-52.

Part 3: Follower

page 110	Compton Cookout: The promotion for the "Compton Cookout" actually occurred in February 2010 at UCSD: www.ktla.com/news/landing/ktla-compton-cookout, 0,2673438.story.
page 113	"a basket of ripe fruit": Amos 8:2.
page 114	"What were you feeling when you saw it?": Psychologist David Benner notes that often the emotive feeling that accompanies dreams (fear, anxiety, joy, peace) is more meaningful than the actual content of the imagery (Sacred Companions [Downers Grove, IL: InterVarsity Press, 2004], pp. 117-18).
page 114	"perfect love casts out fear": 1 John 4:18 NASB.
page 118	"the listening prayer": Though it's hard to beat experiencing it firsthand, I've been helped by the Vineyard Prayer Ministry model, also known as the Five-Step Healing Model, conroevineyard.org/kingdomtools/site/conroevineyard. org/resources/500000000015/Vineyard_Prayer_Ministry_ Model.pdf.
page 120	"He doesn't change": James 1:17.
page 121	"faith isn't about certainty; it's about trust": A nod to Flannery O'Connor who once wrote this to a friend: "Don't expect faith to clear things up for you. It is trust, not certainty." Sally Fitzgerald, ed., *The Habit of Being: Letters of Flannery O'Connor* (New York: Farrar, Straus and Giroux, 1988), p. 354.
page 122	"prophets should speak, and the others should weigh carefully": 1 Corinthians 14:29.

page 123   "when you have sex with someone, it's as if you're married": See 1 Corinthians 6:16.

page 124   "Where two or three are gathered": Matthew 18:20.

page 124   "great cloud of witnesses": Hebrews 12:1.

page 125   "For I am with you": Genesis 26:24; Isaiah 43:5, etc.

page 126   "for strengthening, encouragement and comfort": 1 Corinthians 14:3.

page 126   "quench the Spirit": 1 Thessalonians 5:19.

page 127   fruit of the spirit, a bad tree: Matthew 7:17-19; 12:33; Luke 6:43-44.

page 129   "ongoing conversation with God": Dallas Willard, *Hearing God* (Downers Grove, IL: InterVarsity Press, 1999), p. 18.

page 129   "without individualized communication": Ibid., p. 22.

page 130   "Jesus . . . needed to hear God say that he loved him": Matthew 3:17; 17:5.

page 131   "What is God saying to you?": It's the question Elizabeth Paul asks when she disciples.

page 131   "a person who can weather the storm and a person who can't": Matthew 7:24-27.

page 134   "Faith without deeds is dead": James 2:26.

page 136   Abraham and Isaac: Genesis 22:2, 12.

page 136   "we are called to remain in him": John 15:1-11.

page 136   "if he was persecuted we would be also": John 15:20.

page 140   "the Twelve, the seventy-two, the five hundred": We see the seventy-two in Luke 10:1 and the five hundred in 1 Corinthians 15:6.

Part 4: Leader

pages 151-52 "Come, follow me, and I will send you out to fish for people": Matthew 4:19; Mark 1:17; Luke 5:10.

page 152   "we shouldn't make people leaders too early": See 1 Timothy 3:6.

page 153   the church talking about power in Acts 6: Greek Christians complained that their widows were being overlooked in the daily food distribution. The response by the Jewish apostles was to appoint Greek deacons to be in charge of getting the food out to everyone. They needed to change the power structures between ethnicities, so that all were served. And the result? "So the word of God spread" (Acts 6:7).

page 154   "the ability to successfully introduce a cultural good": Andy Crouch has a great talk titled "Power, Privilege, and Risk" that I highly recommend. You can see it here: www.qideas .org/video/power-privilege-and-risk.aspx. Crouch is currently working on a book on the topic of power and privilege that is forthcoming from InterVarsity Press in 2013 or 2014.

page 155   "Use power, lay down privilege": Ibid.

page 156   the power of his resurrection, the fellowship of his suffering: Philippians 3:10.

page 159   "highest in job satisfaction": Dan Pink discusses our need for autonomy, mastery and purpose to stay motivated in a job. Authority lines up well with autonomy, and if power is about the resources to do a task well, then it lines up well with mastery. Check out his talk, "Dan Pink on the Surprising Science of Motivation": www.ted.com/talks/dan_pink_on_motivation.html.

page 166   "checking all that apply": Sundee Frazier, *Check All That Apply: Finding Wholeness as a Multiracial Person* (Downers Grove, IL: InterVarsity Press, 2001).

page 167   racial categories didn't exist: *Race: The Power of an Illusion*, directed by Larry Adelman (San Francisco: California Newsreel, 2003), DVD.

page 169   Ethnic identity as a biblical identity marker: See James Choung, *True Story: A Christianity Worth Believing In* (Downers Grove, IL: InterVarsity Press, 2008), pp. 99-102. Also check out a video I made with InterVarsity called "Ethnicity Matters," vimeo.com/35721693.

page 170   "the number of multiracial people in this country is climbing": Wendy Wang, "The Rise of Intermarriage: Rates, Characteristics Vary by Race and Gender" (Washington, DC: Pew Social & Demographic Trends, 2012), www.pewsocial trends.org/2012/02/16/the-rise-of-intermarriage/.

page 171   "every tribe, nation, language and tongue": Revelation 7:9.

page 172   "two becoming one": Ephesians 2:14.

Part 5: World Changer

page 180   "UCSD was known as a racist campus": Actual quotes, as reported by Dora Yiu, an InterVarsity staff worker at UCSD, except the names of ministries were changed.

page 180   "I walked away from the church": Ibid.

page 182   "Be salt and light": Matthew 5:13-16.

page 182   "we are world changers": For more, see the chapter titled
                "Why We Can't Change the World" in Andy Crouch, *Culture
                Making* (Downers Grove, IL: InterVarsity Press, 2008), pp.
                187-201.

page 184   "Paul sums up his ministry": 2 Corinthians 5:18.

page 186   "In Scripture, spiritual gifts are": 1 Corinthians 12:7.

page 187   "The place God calls you to": Frederick Buechner, *Wishful
                Thinking: A Theological ABC* (New York: Harper & Row,
                1973), p. 95.

page 187   "What would the kingdom of God": Another question
                pulled from working with Elizabeth Paul.

page 189   "Bible says we're all priests": 1 Peter 2:5-9.

page 189   Rwandan orphans making greeting cards: For more infor-
                mation, check out Cards from Africa at www.cardsfrom
                africa.co.uk.

page 195   "he will crush your head, and you will strike his heel":
                Genesis 3:15.

Walkthrough, Part 1: Skeptic to World Changer

page 217   Walkthrough, Part 1: Much of the material in this
                chapter is adapted from my dissertation, "A Narrative
                Approach to Developing World-Changing Leaders in
                Postmodern Cultures" (DMin diss., Fuller Theological
                Seminary, 2008). You can download it at www.james
                choung.net/dissertation.pdf.

page 218   "do's and don'ts in building trust": Don Everts and Doug
                Schaupp, *I Once Was Lost* (Downers Grove, IL: InterVarsity
                Press, 2008), pp. 33-46.

pages 219-20 "the Big Story could be helpful": The material is best
                found in *True Story: A Christianity Worth Believing In*
                (Downers Grove, IL: InterVarsity Press, 2008). You can also
                find a shorter version for seekers in *Based on a True Story*
                (Downers Grove, IL: InterVarsity Press, 2008), or as a video
                at www.jameschoung.net/2007/09/17/the-big-story.

page 221   "What is God saying to you": Elizabeth Paul, director of
                communications for 3DM.

page 224   "What would the kingdom of God look like": Elizabeth
                Paul, director of communications for 3DM.

ABOUT THE AUTHOR

James Choung seeks to empower rising generations of kingdom world changers. To this end, he currently serves as national director of InterVarsity Asian American Ministries and as pastor of a house church called Vineyard Underground, a network of smaller churches. He is also author of *True Story: A Christianity Worth Believing In* and its companion booklet, *Based on a True Story* (both InterVarsity Press, 2008), which both illustrate how to present Jesus' central message in a way that makes sense to people today. He has taught at Bethel Seminary San Diego on leadership development and evangelism, and he speaks frequently at churches and conferences. His work has been featured in many publications, including *Christianity Today* and *Leadership Journal*.

James wrote his DMin dissertation on postmodern leadership development at Fuller Theological Seminary, received his MDiv from Gordon-Conwell Theological Seminary and studied management science and marketing at MIT. His experience includes serving on the pastoral staff of a Boston-area urban church plant and of a megachurch in Seoul, Korea. He has also led worship at national conferences and has served on boards for higher education and an overseas business startup. For fun, he likes to travel with his wife, tease his two sons, play board games with his buddies, hit some jazzy chords on the keys, enjoy Los Angeles's endless summer and swing a racket in hopes of playing something like tennis. He blogs irregularly at www.jameschoung.net.

Also Available from James Choung
and InterVarsity Press

True Story: A Christianity Worth Believing In

233 pages, paperback, ISBN: 978-0-8308-3609-3

Based on a True Story

32 pages, paperback, ISBN: 978-0-87784-037-4

---

www.ivpress.com

LIKEWISE. *Go and do.*

A man comes across an ancient enemy, beaten and left for dead. He lifts the wounded man onto the back of a donkey and takes him to an inn to tend to the man's recovery. Jesus tells this story and instructs those who are listening to "go and do likewise."

Likewise books explore a compassionate, active faith lived out in real time. When we're skeptical about the status quo, Likewise books challenge us to create culture responsibly. When we're confused about who we are and what we're supposed to be doing, Likewise books help us listen for God's voice. When we're discouraged by the troubled world we've inherited, Likewise books encourage us to hold onto hope.

In this life we will face challenges that demand our response. Likewise books face those challenges with us so we can act on faith.

ivpress.com/likewise
twitter.com/likewise_books
facebook.com/likewisebooks
youtube.com/likewisebooks